In gratitude to Fritz; my teacher.

ISBN: 978-0-9571642-4-6

Page numbers are referenced against the 2004 Harper Perennial edition.

Paperback edition first published in 2015 by R.A. Moseley.
This second revised edition first published in 2018.

This paperback has been produced by Create Space.

Contents

Contents (contd.)

Part I: Introduction

The Lost Art of Discipleship

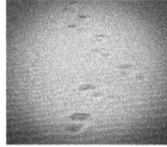

Dr Fritz Schumacher was a man who spent his life breaking free of the 'package' that he was born and raised into. In this sense he was controversial; as he quietly refused to follow the crowd and instead walked his own way. Born in Germany in 1911, during a dark time in this country's history, he knew that he had to break free of this package and moved to England in the 1930's. Both here and in America he was educated into a system of conventional economic belief...and he also had to break free of this package.

In walking his own way, Schumacher established himself in the fields of energy, agriculture, ecology, and economic development during a distinguished career. But his reputation was not built on his grasp of abstract concepts and formulas but on his realisation that *people mattered*. The human factor was central to his life and work but his was not a psychology of helping sick people become 'normal'. Instead his passion lay in helping 'normal' people blossom and grow into the fullness of their potential. His teaching was personal and intimately directed at the heart of the individual. Although he is best known for his publication, Small is Beautiful, it was in his final work, A Guide for the Perplexed, that Schumacher offered the heart of his teaching and, to my mind, revealed himself as the true mystic that he was.

As Schumacher broke free of his package, this small book is about you and about the importance of breaking free of your 'package'... whatever it may be. In a sense it will appear to be quite negative in tone for one who is comfortable and happy in his package will never break free of it. If Schumacher had grown up in a rural idyll instead of a Germany that was in a state of deep unease he may never have left.

In the beginning though we need to take a *look at our package* rather than simply accept what we have been told about it. For it is in looking at the package we have inherited that we learn to think for ourselves...and it is in learning to think for ourselves that we begin to know thyself. Only then are we ready to ascend and to begin the truly religious life. Schumacher himself explains the process:

> *Taking our bearings from the four Great Truths discussed in this book and studying the interconnections between these four landmarks on our 'map,' we do not find it difficult to discern what constitutes true progress of a human being:*
>
> *1) One's first task is to learn from society and 'tradition' and to find one's temporary happiness in receiving directions from outside.*
>
> *2) One's second task is to interiorize the knowledge one has gained, sift it, sort it out, keeping the good, jettisoning the bad; this process may be called 'individuation,' becoming self-directed.*
>
> *3) One's third task cannot be tackled until one has accomplished the first two, and is one for which one needs the very best help that can possibly be found: It is 'dying to oneself,' to one's likes and dislikes, to all one's egocentric preoccupations. To the extent that one succeeds in this, one ceases to be directed from outside, and also ceases to be self-directed. One has gained freedom or, one might say, one is then God-directed. If one is a Christian, that is precisely what one would hope to say.*

> *Schumacher, A Guide for the Perplexed, p.135.*

It is in his final piece of work that Schumacher begins to work on one package in particular in sifting it, sorting it out, keeping the good and jettisoning the bad. This package is one of the biggest that we in our modern western culture have inherited - namely the package of scientific materialism – and he reveals how lost we have become on the map of life because of it. From there Schumacher offers many pointers to help us undertake the third task that lies before us and which must be taken alone.

This book is my honest attempt to pay homage to this important teaching and to bring his Guide for the Perplexed into your awareness again.

It was difficult though to know how best to approach the task. I knew that I didn't want to try and rehash the book for the sake of rehashing it and I don't think my words can convey any better the wisdom that Fritz Schumacher was communicating. I also find myself in a very different circumstance to that faced by Joseph Pearce in his endeavour to update Small is Beautiful in 2001 and to bring it up to date and into context with our current situation and time. Deep down I know that Schumacher's Guide for the Perplexed embodies a timeless piece of wisdom that needs no updating and it applies to mankind today as equally well as it could have applied to mankind two-thousand years ago.

So what I decided to do instead is to approach this homage to the Guide by speaking about the *lost art of discipleship*. In this small book I will be seeking to illuminate how the student must strive to become adequate in order to truly hear what is being taught by their teacher rather than weakly bringing the teaching down to their current lower level of understanding.

In essence there has always been the struggle that is faced by the one who has gone beyond to the other shore and who has to communicate what it is they have seen. Their teaching has inevitably been misunderstood and misused by those who eagerly follow and yet fail to learn and grasp the art of true discipleship. Never has there been a time in human history when more than a small minority have been able to grasp the wisdom teachings that have been handed down to us. But if our civilisation is to thrive in this world then this lost art is one that we all truly need to master…and we need to master it now.

I begin this book with a few words about my own personal story and background and how my desire to become a disciple of the teaching emerged and blossomed. From there I will then share with you a personal letter from a disciple to his teacher; a letter that provided the impetus for beginning this work.

Then I will offer a series of meditations on the Guide itself. In the Harper Perennial 2004 edition that I own there are 140 pages, and I attuned to a different page each day and a section of text from that page. I then spent one hour a day over a period of forty days in contemplation on the words I was given to work with. Sometimes I surprised myself with what emerged during this precious time I spent in the company of the teacher each morning; and sometimes I was surprised how one meditation led seamlessly onto the next.

However, the words that emerged in this time of contemplation are not necessarily of value or interest. Instead, what I am trying to do with these meditations is to illuminate the *process* that one has to go through in order to get on the same wavelength of the teacher and his or her teaching. For it is in this quiet time of contemplation that the disciple may uncover the jewel of the teaching that transforms their life completely. It is in this quiet time of contemplation that we may begin to accept the invitation of awakening that the genuine master always puts before us. It is in this quiet time of contemplation that we may learn to truly practice and master this lost art of discipleship.

Answering the Call: My Own Personal Story

It was in the early summer of 1996 that I first recall Fritz Schumacher's presence within me as I felt, and responded, to the strong call inside to choose the field of Economics as one of my subjects of study at sixth-form College. It was a pure 'leftfield' decision – for it was not a subject I knew anything about; except perhaps a vague notion that it had something to do with money. I also remember it being a strange choice given that I'd not even enjoyed the Business Studies course I'd taken at High School. However, having responded to this call, I eventually pursued my interest in this field right through into university where I received a Bachelor of Science for my efforts.

But although I had a passion for the subject; throughout these six years I felt a distinct and growing unease with what I was being taught. Deep down I knew that the whole science of economics was being built on an assumption which if taken away would bring it crashing down like a house of cards. This assumption was *homo economicus* – the assumption that there is nothing more to man than the rational workings of his own conscious mind. The fundamental unanswered question I was left with at the end of this period was:

What would our economy look like if man was living in soul rather than ego consciousness?

I felt alone in my unease and, bizarrely, it seemed to me as if none of my fellow students or tutors had ever considered such a question or had ever thought to challenge this underlying assumption. It seemed as if having *homo economicus* around made their science easier to define and more comfortable to predict with its straight line logic and rationality. However, in the March of 2003, some nine months after leaving university, I discovered for the first time that I hadn't really been alone in asking this question and that, surprisingly, there had been one economist who'd been exploring this right throughout the twentieth century. Through Joseph Pearce's wonderful book, Small is Still Beautiful, I heard for the first time the name of Fritz Schumacher. In this discovery I realised that Schumacher's book, Small is Beautiful, captured all the issues I'd been concerned about in my studies. He appeared to be the one economist who was troubled by the same questions as I'd been, and who had the answers and the foresight to express a practical vision of how our economy could function if man was indeed living in soul consciousness. After reading this book I soon realised that there were in fact many people who have been inspired by this vision, and I also discovered that, despite the academic world snubbing his name and work, outside of their radar there had been a lot of positive changes taking place.

With this I quickly became enthused with a passion for economic reform as I explored many different avenues for bringing about change so as to try and do my bit in helping to create a more perfect world that expressed the best of who we are in soul consciousness. In doing so I especially became involved in the environmental sector, in community regeneration, and in land-use planning. I even made concrete plans for my own business that was going to be operated on new economic principles; but it couldn't be financed.

However it was on one afternoon spent scanning through the bookshelves of Birmingham Library in 2006 that I came upon another book that would change things significantly for me. This was Schumacher's later book; A Guide for the Perplexed. I was surprised to see it because although I'd become an avid follower of his work I'd not even been aware that a second book had been written. I also remember being especially struck by the fact that this had been published in 1977, the last year of his life. It soon became clear to me that this book offered the final full flowering of his consciousness.

The book changed things significantly for me because what I

discovered through reading it – not overnight but gradually over the next few years – was the realisation that my endeavours for economic reform were going to fail because they were coming from the mind of fear rather than the heart of love. With this realisation I began to live my life more and more from my heart and I slowly released my ego's obsession with trying to fix the world of its problems.

I was able to do this because as well as having an passion for new economics, like Schumacher, I had also become interested in the religious life after leaving university. My studies had shown me the soulless world that I was living in, and as much as I was trying to change my environment, I was also in search of something *inside of myself* that would fill the vacuum. I had travelled the world and been inspired to see ancient cultures that were still rooted in the land and in spirit, and, like Schumacher, I developed an interest in Buddhism and eastern teachings as I made my own journey into the ways of the spirit.

However I eventually saw that Buddhism was just another label and another abstract mental concept; and that I had to go deeper still into the real and direct experience of the religious life. On this continuing journey I am always surprised to find that whenever I gain insights and take a step forward in my life that I find evidence of Schumacher's footprints. It is as if he has walked this same road before; and whenever I can track his footsteps I immediately feel reassured that I must be heading in the right direction.

So it is through my explorations into the religious life that I am now able to get more of an understanding of what Schumacher means when he says in the Guide that the true revolution must come from the inside out rather than the outside in. I am starting to finally step more comfortably into the shoes of discipleship and to become adequate to the 'true teaching' that is being offered.

He is the role model for me of someone who had dedicated his life to solving economic problems; but who came to the humbling realisation towards the end of his life that in truth there were *no economic problems to solve*. He knew then, as I do now, that the real root problem of mankind was a religious one and that this is where the work of transformation and change really needs to take place. I am so grateful that I was able to realise this piece of wisdom in my twenties without having to go through a lengthy career in the field as he had to do. I also feel that his efforts over the sixty six years of his life has indeed made the situation a lot easier for those who follow him and who do not go have to go through and learn the same lessons as he did. What a gift this is for those of us who keep finding evidence of footsteps that helps us from straying off the path.

A Letter from a Disciple to his Teacher

Although I have committed myself as your disciple in private I do feel daunted by the task of making my discipleship public. It is one thing to put your words of wisdom into practice in my own life but I have to ask myself: *by what authority can I dare to take on the responsibility of writing this book?* Not only that but I also have to ask myself; *why am I alone in feeling so strongly that your teaching has not been heard and grasped and that the art of discipleship hasn't been practiced by many who have tried to follow in your footsteps?*

I have doubts because surely there are others who *know you* more intimately than I do and who are better equipped to decide whether there is something to be spoken here. For one thing our paths never crossed and my time on this earth began three years after yours had ended. Nor have I researched your biography in any great depth to claim that I know you in that personal sense. I am also not an established name and figure of expertise in the fields of interest that you concerned yourself with and I don't have any bestsellers to my name to call myself a successful writer.

Yet despite these doubts in my mind here I am. Deep down I know that all I have that qualifies me for the task is a longing in my heart. Even deeper down I know that this is all that matters. For as a teacher you were the one who pointed the way home and I know that I heard this not in words but as a *feeling* in my heart. It comes to me as the quiet whisper of your own beating heart; and it is this whisper which helps to stir and wake up my own heartfelt longing to awaken and return home. This feels intimate and brings me closer than close to you. Surely this whisper is the only thing the willing disciple needs to listen out for in order to really hear the teaching of the master?

What I felt in this whisper was something that is truly timeless and ageless. What I felt was the passing down of a lineage of wisdom that came through you. I know now that it was not personal to you and did not arise out of the story of your biography; it is a jewel that was present inside of you all along. Like it was there inside of you, I know that it is also there inside of all of us waiting to emerge. From a Christian perspective I also sense that this ageless whisper first emerged into the world in the Gospels when Matthew and Luke recorded the following commands of Jesus Christ[1]:

'But seek ye first the kingdom of God, and his righteousness, and all else shall be added unto you.'

Matthew (vi.33)

'The kingdom of God cometh not with outward show; neither shall they say, Lo here! or, Lo there! for behold, the kingdom of God is within you'

Luke (xvii. 20, 21)

I know that there are many great souls who have taken these words to heart over the years and who allowed it to transform their lives; and the lives of those around them. You too followed in the footsteps of this lineage and responded to the commands in your life and work.

I sense that in this day and age, and perhaps more so than at any other time in human history, it is critical that more and more people take these words to heart. For ours is a time, especially in the western world, where we continue to hold on stubbornly to the opposite. Out of fear we are told to make sure that we put bread on the table first, and then, perhaps in our spare time, or most likely towards the end of our life, we can

---

[1] The translation for these commands came from Leo Tolstoy's, The Kingdom of God is Within You (1894)

go ahead and look for the kingdom. Even in this so-called modern age we find ourselves dedicating the best part of our lives to economic survival rather than something higher. Even now we simply haven't got our priorities straight and our relationships remained strained to say the least. Not only the relationships with those closest to us but also the relationship we have with the world as a whole.

I feel there is a sense of urgency in restating the teaching once more. However, the urgency does not come through me because I read of dire warnings about the state of our world and our civilisation. The urgency comes instead because of my close observations over the years of those people who are busily engaged in a process of economic reform and who are essentially putting your teachings into practice *in the name of discipleship*. It is for these people that I feel pressed to write with this sense of urgency because their efforts have taken us along a new and misguided direction. It may have been destined to happen this way but when I see that the path clearly lies straight ahead, and then see well-intentioned people hesitate and take a turn to the right or to the left, I simply cannot stand back in silence.

This book is truly a reminder that the time has come for us take courage and to walk on. I am aware though that in bringing up these commands again that they come with a strong word of warning which may not be comfortable for the reader to hear.

For why is it that our courage is failing and that all these well-intentioned people are choosing instead to take a detour? I think we are struggling to take that path straight ahead because I sense that it leaves many of us feeling somewhat queasy to realise that we can achieve peace and permanence in our economies; that we can live in a world of meaningful work within human-scale organisations; that we can eradicate poverty in our own communities and in the developing world; that we can achieve sustainability of energy production and consumption; that we can establish a respectful relationship with the natural world...and yet despite all of this find it possible that we are still lost when locating our position against the four landmarks on the map which you give for us in the Guide.

This is because the four landmarks on the map in the Guide are about us and are not about the world. They are very intimate and very personal and it is because it is so close to touching our hearts that we push it far, far away. Deep down I think many of us would much rather live with our ideas, concepts and formulas of peace than to make it real in our hearts. We would much rather take a detour and tinker with the systems of the world and with the lives of our neighbours than to take the walk and find the kingdom within.

Yes I know you were a practical man who would not have discouraged the actions that have been taken to create a fairer and more sustainable economic system. There has been much progress since your death, in the UK at least, and it is not for me to say that there is not goodness to be found in this work. But what I can say is that there is a risk we are creating for ourselves a new herd of sacred cows to honour and worship as the means continue to be confused for the ends. There is a risk that in taking that detour that we are still pouring our energies into putting bread on the table rather than in seeking the kingdom that lies inside. We both know that if these reforms continue to be carried out without understanding the essence and wisdom of your teaching that they will fail to achieve the lasting change and revolution (or homecoming as you would perhaps call it) of mankind that you yearned for.

It is this feeling of queasiness that I am sure I will be returning to a lot in this book and I think it is our own discomfort around taking that leap of faith and staying true to the path that explains why the Guide only sold a relatively small number of copies and was discontinued. In contrast the earlier publication, Small is Beautiful, has sold more than a million copies and continues to remain a popular and influential title today. To my mind these facts reveal something about where we are at as a civilisation. For it is possible (though not encouraged by you) to read Small is Beautiful and to keep our focus on changing and reforming the world 'out there' without having to looking inwards at ourselves. In the absence of religion this has become an inevitable habit that we've acquired because whilst we have developed the capacity to affect our environment around us; we simply don't have the skills anymore to work with our own inner landscape.

But though the picture appears gloomy; now is not the moment

13

to lose hope and all I can do is to point the way home for those who are ready to receive direction. May I find the resolve to keep my eyes firmly on the kingdom and may I turn to these final words of your Guide to stay steadfast in this important work:

> Can we rely on it that a 'turning around' will be accomplished by enough people quickly enough to save the modern world? The question is often asked, but no matter what the answer, it will mislead. The answer 'Yes' would lead to complacency, the answer 'No' to despair. It is desirable to leave these perplexities behind us and get down to work.

> Schumacher, A Guide for the Perplexed, p.140.

Part II: Meditations on A Guide for the Perplexed

Grades of Significance

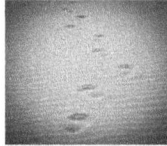

In the Fourth Field of Knowledge[2] there is only observation of movement and other kinds of material change; meaning or purpose, intelligence or chance, freedom or necessity, as well as life, consciousness and self-awareness cannot be sensually observed. Only 'signs' can be found and observed; the observer has to choose the *grade of significance* he is willing to attribute to them.

Schumacher, A Guide for the Perplexed, p.110.

Can I taste meaning with my tongue? Can I touch freedom with my fingers? Can I see purpose with my eyes? Can I smell necessity with my nose? Can I hear intelligence with my ears?

Let us think about this together for a moment. Can it really be true that the depth of our life experience depends on the quantity and quality of data received through our five senses? Do we really need to rely on outer stimulants to bring meaning to our lives? Is it not possible to have a rich life experience without any stimulation; at a time when there is no data to be sensually observed?

This is what we are here to explore together in the first meditation.

---

[2] The Fourth Field of Knowledge is defined as: "the appearance of the world around us. By appearance I mean everything that offers itself to our senses...the decisive question is always 'what do I actually observe?'" (Schumacher, A Guide for the Perplexed, p.100).

16

I feel we need to look at the field of language and communication as an example here. We can go to a foreign speaking country and in a matter of weeks or months learn the signs of language that need to be observed and mimicked in order to function in that country. Yet I've heard from those who've done it that it can take many months, or possibly years, before they can truly 'hear' and experience genuine communication with another person in that country. For what our training in the language cannot give us is the feelings that are being communicated from beyond the words and which can only be intuited through experience. What is missing is the quality of empathy; which in this instance adds a richer qualitative dimension to our relationships. It defines for us a higher grade of significance. And when this quality of empathy emerges with another person, especially when in a foreign speaking country, it is typically felt as an experience of spiritual illumination that has descended by an act of grace. This is because it brings in that quality of mutual understanding which in its absence often leaves us feeling alienated and bereft.

Yet is it not the case for many of us that we have become obsessed with observing and mimicking behaviour? It seems as if the ability to function in the world is our utmost priority and we walk around holding tightly to our language guidebooks. Of course the Fourth Field of Knowledge has its place and it is not wise to dismiss the value of being a functional human being in the world. But does it not feel too constricting to limit ourselves to this when there is this possibility of something richer to be experienced. Are we not denying who we truly are as human beings when we close ourselves off to these experiences of grace?

It is, though, a conundrum for us because we cannot control when the experience of grace will descend. It doesn't seem as if it is dependent on our efforts and no matter how well we master the language it is, in truth, as liable to descend on the holiday tourist who knows only two words as the scholar who has been learning and practicing the language for years. There is therefore a risk involved when taking the chance to open ourselves to the possibility that there might be something richer to be experienced here. We risk being disappointed and for this reason we cling to what is known. We cling to the visible signs to be observed and shut ourselves off from any higher grades of significance. Is this not the case? Is this not what we have been trained to do?

So this brings us to the question of whether we have any free will or not. In truth it is both all up to us and all up to grace. To function in the world is valuable in itself and mastering the Fourth Field of Knowledge is valuable in itself. It is healthy to observe the visible signs. It is all up to us. It is also true that we have free will to choose the grade of significance. We can have the belief that there is nothing more to experience than the visible signs or we can have the belief that there is so much more going on here. It is all up to us.

Yet what is hard for us is that if we believe that there is nothing but the visible signs then our experience will confirm this belief because we will never ever catch the moment of grace should it happen to descend. We were therefore right to have this belief and the cycle is reinforced. However, if we believe that there is more then we may or may not be right because our belief doesn't necessarily mean that we will experience grace; it just means that we are more likely to catch it should it ever happen to descend. But if it does descend, and if we do catch it, then our lives will never truly be the same again.

So what do you choose to do? Do you play it safe or do you take a risk?

The Invisible Powers

The Great Truth of '*adaequatio*' affirms that nothing can be perceived without an appropriate organ of perception and that nothing can be understood without an appropriate organ of understanding. For cognition at the mineral level, man's primary instruments are his five senses, reinforced and extended by a great array of ingenious apparatus. They register the visible world, but cannot register the 'inwardness' of things and such fundamental invisible powers as life, consciousness and self-awareness. Who could see, hear, touch, taste or smell *life as such*?

Schumacher, A Guide for the Perplexed, p.50.

We have been exploring together whether we can open ourselves to the possibility of a richer life experience by becoming less reliant on observations made through our five senses. This naturally leads us to the question of where this capacity of openness is located inside of us. What part of our being allows us to experience this special quality of empathy that we have already spoken about?

The quality of empathy seems to emerge whenever we fully utilise the invisible powers of life, consciousness and self-awareness. Yet no scientist has ever been able to pinpoint where these powers lie within us or how to create these powers from scratch. For the scientist can only perceive and understand things at the mineral level and can only register what is happening in the visible world.

So how do we know in ourselves that we are alive when there is no visible or tangible on-off switch that we can go to and check? There is no way of proving that we have this gift of life within us. We can only tell that we have it in comparison with its absence. We can know when this gift of life is absent because we can observe from the visible signs that it is missing. How interesting is this? It is science by the process of decay rather than the process of creation.

The same is true for the additional powers of consciousness and self-awareness and it is through the latter that we can know ourselves that we are experiencing empathy. We may have a sense that it occurs in the heart region and we may feel a warming sensation here whenever it happens to arise.

Does it not seem unwise therefore to deny the validity of our own inner experience of empathy just because we are told that it is not verifiable? Are we not living in an impoverished world by not consciously recognising these invisible powers within us and by not activating them to their fullest potential?

It brings me to the matter of healing and the problem in our civilisation of relying on what we know through our five senses to cure our ailments. We hear consistently of people healing themselves from incurable diseases and yet fail to validate that this is solely because these individuals have a certain degree of faith in their own invisible powers to bring about healing.

So when choosing to open ourselves to a higher grade of significance we are not merely doing so to give our two-dimensional lives more colour and body through the experience of grace. For are we not trying to tread this path in order to cultivate and hone our inner powers so that we live our lives more fully as self-aware and conscious human beings? Because if we accept the Great Truth of adaequatio, then denying the possibility that there are higher grades of significance will surely cause these powers to lie dormant and neglected inside of us. If we believe that there is nothing more than can be perceived through the five senses; then the five senses will be the only organs of perception and understanding that we will use.

Is this neglect the biggest regret that people face at the end of their life? For as the visible form of our life begins to fade away do we not see begin to see more clearly the untended wasteland of our invisible world?

But why do we have to wait for our visible world to fade before we can see what is truly important for us? Why do we have to wait to see our untended wasteland at the time of death when it is too late to do our inner gardening work? Why do we have to get really sick before we can develop faith in our own inner powers and in our capacity to heal?

The Modern Experiment

> It may conceivably be possible to live without churches; but it is
> not possible to live without religion, that is, without systematic
> work to keep in contact with, and develop toward, Higher Levels
> than those of 'ordinary life' with all its pleasure or pain, sensa-
> tion, gratification, refinement or crudity – whatever it may be.
> *The modern experiment to live without religion has failed*, and
> once we have understood this, we know what our 'post modern'
> tasks really are.

Schumacher, A Guide for the Perplexed, p.139.

It feels as if we are starting to move even deeper together into this
field of distinction between the experience of 'ordinary life' and our
experiences of Higher Levels of being.

When we talk here of ordinary life it strikes me that we are speaking solely about the outer appearance and expression of who we are in
ego consciousness. This is what we call economics. Of course we need to
establish for ourselves a healthy and fully functional personality in ego
consciousness. It seems to me that it is not wise to abandon and neglect
this aspect of who we are and to live in a state of inner dysfunction and
turmoil. And as we need to live a healthy life in ego consciousness so we
need to live a healthy economic life. Whereas economics is about getting
our outer house in order; the ego is about getting our inner house in
order. The former is but a reflection of the latter.

So when we live an ordinary life we are trying to get the best deal for ourselves. We are trying to get our lives sorted so that we are a smoothly running and highly efficient organism. Our goal in life is to maximise our experience of pleasure and to minimise our experience of pain. Our goal in life is to always stay that one step ahead of death and annihilation. When we live an ordinary life we are trying to stay in control and to keep ourselves firmly in the driving seat.

But we need to ask ourselves whether this very modern experiment has failed. Has the pursuit of these goals truly brought us any real and lasting satisfaction? The desire and obsession to get our own inner and outer houses in order shows itself in many different forms. Yet all of the forms have at the root an inherent restlessness and dissatisfaction regardless of whether order can be achieved or not. We have over time trod over a million different paths to bring about this experience of order and control over our environment and each path has led nowhere. We have tried communism, capitalism, environmentalism, socialism, fundamentalism, nihilism, scientism, animalism, sectarianism – and all the other 'isms' you can think of. All these paths, and many, many more, have at their root a desire to bring about reformation from the outside in. They all desire to achieve a better economic order that reflects the individual's own inner order.

And of course what we think will bring about order to our own inner world is different for each individual. We are all the manifestation of many different conditions and circumstances and it is the combination of these that makes us unique. Our gender, our race, our family background, our culture, our education, our life experience all comes together to help form and mould our own unique belief system. They all come together to help form our sense of ourselves and our world. Many of us then spend our lives struggling to create an economic order that mirrors our own unique inner sense of order. Competition and conflict ensues with others who share different beliefs and the root sense of dissatisfaction and restlessness does not disappear. Even if we manage to get our own way and achieve an economic order that is in perfect harmony with our own inner order…it will never be sustained.

This was the modern experiment that was always doomed to fail.

This was the modern experiment that attempted to create an 'economic' order that everyone agreed with and accepted. This is the best outcome that could be hoped for by those who want to do the best for humanity but who, nevertheless, are bound by the limited rules of ordinary life. Whilst these souls may be acting with the right desire there can be no love, wisdom or compassion in their actions.

But how does this inform us of what our post-modern tasks really are? If the modern experiment to live without religion has truly failed then this takes us onto shaky ground for we seem to have become confused as to what religion really is. For many of us religion is just another 'ism' that has tried and failed to bring about economic order to our world. We are rightly wary of a religion that becomes just one more condition that moulds our belief system. We are rightly wary of a religion that is preached to us by those who are bound by the limited rules of ordinary life and who cannot see beyond them.

Yet the true religious life can take us beyond our conditions and beyond our belief system altogether. It can take us beyond our ordinary life and in touch with the Higher Levels. Religion in truth is a practice, is a way of life, which does indeed help us to develop a relationship and stay in contact with those Higher Levels of being.

So having had an experience of grace, and having recognised that there is more to who we are than ego consciousness, it seems as if our post modern task is to find our religious practice and to practice it so that this experience of grace does not simply descend upon us again by chance.

The Greatest Sin

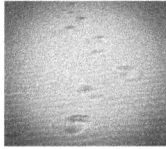

In spite of the modern world's chaos and its suffering, there is hardly a concept more unacceptable to it than the idea of sin. What could be the meaning of sin anyhow? Traditionally it means 'missing the mark,' as in archery, missing the very purpose of human life on earth, a life that affords unique opportunities for development, a great chance and privilege, as the Buddhists have it, 'hard to obtain.' Whether tradition speaks the truth or not cannot be decided by any 'science for manipulation'; it can be decided only by those highest faculties of man which are *adequate* to the creation of a 'science for understanding.' If the very possibility of the latter is systematically denied, the highest faculties are never brought into play, they atrophy, and the very possibility of first understanding and then fulfilling the purpose of life disappears.

Schumacher, A Guide for the Perplexed, p.60.

What I observe as interesting from this quote is that the second part appears to refer to something totally separate from the first. But let us look at this more deeply together to get a sense of whether there is a connection to be found.

For the first part of the quote speaks of the concept of sin. It has been observed by many writers that this concept has been used historically in a very negative and limiting way. Sin has been used un-lovingly to cast judgment down upon another person's shoulders and it weighs as a heavy burden upon it. It has a patriarchal scolding quality associated with it. Yet when sin is defined more honestly as having simply missed the mark, the heavy weight it carries seems to melt. To acknowledge either your own, or someone else's, sin becomes a more motherly and caring act. To live in harmonious relationship with the concept of sin means that we let go of our desire to have things all fully worked out and we let go of our hang-ups about trying to live with some idolised image of perfection. Then the rare quality of humility can sometimes emerge in the midst of the world's chaos and its suffering.

But in this meditation we are looking more deeply into the root of sin. We are looking at the greatest sin of all which is to miss the very purpose of human life on earth. Out of this all other sins surely emerge for one who is very clear and focused about their purpose of human life on earth will be less likely to stray and deviate off the path in the details of day-to-day living. They will not be as troubled and caught up in the chaos and suffering of the world and will live their lives with more assurance in who they are and in what they are here to do.

So the greatest sin is our belief that we can live in a world without religion; namely the systematic work to stay in contact with and develop toward Higher Levels than those of ordinary life. There is a famous quote by the Sufi poet Rumi who reminds us, somewhat humorously, that we have been sent to this earth to fulfil one task and yet we often spend our lives busy fulfilling a multitude of other tasks and forgetting the one thing we are here for. This is the ultimate sin that we commit for ourselves.

That one task that we are here to fulfil as human beings is to love. Do we know in ourselves that as human beings we are afforded this unique opportunity to develop and practice love? But what do we mean here by love? Love is nothing other than mindful and transcendent awareness, which is exactly what we need to cultivate through our religious practice. This awareness takes us beyond the drama of our lives to what is real and enduring. Love takes us beyond words.

So how does the ultimate sin that we commit connect with what is spoken in the second part of the quote? What is science for manipulation as it is termed here? In ourselves can we see that when we use the observations we receive through our five senses to control our environment and our lives that we are employing science for manipulation? It is an issue of education. Most of my own schooling was geared towards science for manipulation. During my own upbringing I was taught how to observe my environment, and in the name of science, I was shown the tools I could use to control and manipulate it. It was not only the natural environment that I was given the tools of manipulation but the human environment too. For the knowledge I gained gave me great powers...but I was never given the training on how to use those powers wisely and was only encouraged to use them cunningly in ways that manipulated others. I was left bereft of wisdom by my teachers. It was of no surprise to me to see many of my university colleagues heading off to work in the financial sector and eventually creating this heavy burden of chaos and suffering which we saw blossom when the financial system started to unravel. This is what inevitably happens when relying solely on the science for manipulation.

So I knew that there surely could be no love arising from my actions when these actions were being formed by my observations alone. Only chaos and suffering can ensue from this. For love has to arise from wisdom; and wisdom is something that surely emerges as a higher quality from beyond our observations. It is our wisdom that determines whether something is true or not. Wisdom is a quality that is termed here as science for understanding.

We have it in us to become more than adequate to the task of creating a science for understanding. Yet if we do not employ our faculties to the fullest then our adequateness will atrophy. So if the ultimate sin is that we forget our purpose for being here, which is to love, then the cause of this sin lies in the act of betrayal of our own inner faculties. Yes our upbringing may not support us in developing our faculties but ultimately it is all up to us. We have to find it in ourselves.

It is not at all possible to remember our purpose for being here unless we fully realise our potential for understanding. It is not at all possible to fulfil our purpose of love without the prior wisdom of understanding.

So we are going even deeper now into the root of the matter. If the creation of a science of understanding is the one salvation left for us, and if our religious practice is the one thing that can give this gift to us, then how do we find our practice?

Bare Attention

Bare Attention is attainable only by stopping, or, if it cannot be stopped, calmly observing all 'inner chatter.' It stands *above* thinking, reasoning, arguing, forming opinions – these essential yet subsidiary activities which classify, connect, and verbalise the insights obtained through Bare Attention.

Schumacher, A Guide for the Perplexed, p.70.

Having left the fourth meditation with the question of how to find our practice we turn now to the Buddhist practice of Right Mindfulness. It marks the beginning of the beginning and one starting point for religious practice. It is about stopping the habitual wheel from turning inexorably onwards. Namely the habit we have in our minds of reacting to the information we receive through our observations and of trying to make sense of the jumble of information that passes through our brains.

This is the inner chatter that is constantly arising within us.

So the practice of Right Mindfulness helps us to take that step back and disassociate ourselves from the chatter. It is about cultivating that quality of inner self awareness that allows us to take a much broader view and to see that our identity cannot be confined and defined by this chatter. There is more to who we are than our chatter.

But how do we take that step back? One observation I'd make is that our ambition is not to make our mind quiet. It is possible to train a mind to behave as it is possible to train a dog to be obedient; but there is no love in this relationship. There is too much rigidity and seriousness in our approach when we try to get our mind to behave in this manner. Instead what we need to do is to simply allow the chatter to blow itself out by not fuelling it with our attention. If we can stand back and calmly observe the chatter its hold over us will diminish.

It is like a child of ours who is misbehaving and playing up because it is trying to get our attention. It is not a very loving approach to constantly drop everything else to mollycoddle the child and to give the attention they are seeking. It is not a very loving or sustainable approach to do this in order to get the child to be quiet and to behave nicely. Instead we sometimes need to just stay calm, take that step back out of the drama of the situation, and to discover that the child's tantrums will soon pass. Of course we have to be careful not to go to the other extreme and simply ignore the child and hope that they will eventually shut up. This is not the practice either. With bare attention we simply learn how to stay present and to observe what is arising without reacting to it. It is through the power of our loving presence that the situation blows over.

But is it not part of everyday human activity to think, reason, argue and form opinions? Is our inner chatter not a useful tool for us in making sense of the jumble and chaos of our experiences? Yes absolutely it is a useful tool for us. We are not trying to stop the thinking process altogether. Much of the modern world that we live in was manifested out of our cognitive intelligence and a lot of it serves a purpose in making our lives more ordered, efficient and practical. It is not thinking that is the problem here but the identification we hold with our thinking. We believe that we are our thoughts and we believe that the 'I' is the part of us that is bringing some sort of inner order and structure through our thinking.

Yet this 'I' is nothing more than a servant to a higher power and force that rests inside of us. It carries out subsidiary activities of thinking and reasoning but it doesn't have the power to determine and discern where its services are most needed.

It is only in stopping the habitual wheel from turning that this higher power and force can emerge from inside of us. Out of the busyness of our mental chatter we can create these gaps of stillness and silence where moments of genuine insight and clarity can emerge. Often it is just an intuitive hunch that appears in our mind as if from nowhere and it is through our Bare Attention that we begin to hear and distinguish its voice from the rest of our mental chatter.

When we have reached this point our religious practice has truly begun.

Beyond Logic

The pairs of opposites, of which, freedom and order and growth and decay are the most basic, put tension into the world, a tension that sharpens man's sensitivity and increases his self-awareness. No real understanding is possible without awareness of these pairs of opposites which permeate everything man does... (Yet) our logical mind does not like them: it generally operates on the either/or or yes/no principle, like a computer. So, at any time it wishes to give its exclusive allegiance to either one or the other of the pair, and since this exclusiveness inevitably leads to an ever more loss of realism and truth, the mind may suddenly change sides, often without even noticing it. It swings like a pendulum from one opposite to the other, and each time there is a feeling of 'making up one's mind afresh'; or the mind may become rigid and lifeless, fixing itself on one side of the pair of opposites and feeling that now 'the problem has been solved.'

Schumacher, A Guide for the Perplexed, p.127.

Having explored the limitations that arise when we identify ourselves with our inner chatter in the fifth meditation; we need to begin moving more deeply into this field of exploration. For not only do we fail to access the fullness of our inner faculties and harm ourselves in the process; but we also cause harm to others.

Ours is the age of relationship for it is only in relationship that the love that is locked inside of us can emerge and flourish. Let us remind ourselves that our single purpose for being on this planet is to love. Yet our relationship with ourselves and with others is marred and hindered when we only draw upon the resources of our inner mental chatter. The conclusions we form out of our thinking and reasoning are too blunt and simplistic to create harmonious and loving relationships with others. Only conflict and despair can arise when our interactions with others are formed out of these conclusions.

We may be able to draw on our logic and reasoning when relating to a piece of wood that we wish to shape into a different form. Science for manipulation, as already defined, is perfectly suitable for this task because the block of wood has no inner qualities of life, consciousness and self-awareness that we need to relate with. It is only the visible physical form of the wood that we are in relationship with and in relationship with physical forms we can operate in a very simplistic and mechanistic way. We can employ computers to answer the question for us of how to change the block of wood into a different form.

But when we start to move into relationship with plants and animals, and then beyond that with human beings, we need to be a little more careful and respectful of the non-visible dimensions of existence. Plants are different to a block of wood in that they have this quality we call life added to them. Animals are different again in that as well as life they have this quality we call consciousness added to them. Then humans are different again in that as well as life and consciousness they have this quality we call self-awareness added to them. Human beings are the most difficult to relate with because they act according to their own inner conscious will and are not directed by external forces. It is impossible to control another human being unless they give you their permission for it. In contrast you can control a block of wood without any need for permission.

It is because human beings can act according to their own inner conscious will that there is a tension in the world. Rules of logic are thrown out of the window and we need to develop new skills in order to create loving and harmonious relationships. For our lives are permeated by living problems that simply cannot be nailed down by our reasoning and that we are invited to grapple with on a daily basis.

Yet unless we hone our inner faculties to meet and grow with these living problems, we will either rigidly hold on to one extreme position of untruth or we will jump from one to the other and become lost in a mist of confusion.

But why do these living problems arise for humanity alone? Is it not because life is bigger than logic and that to a certain degree we as human beings have freedom of inner experience? One person can read a book and have one inner experience and another person can read the same book and have a different experience? Is this not why we have different schools of thought *within* all of our religions? Is this not the cause of all human conflict in the world?

The problem does not lie in having this range and divergence of inner experiences but the problem is how to establish harmonious and loving relationships within them. When someone has an inner experience and, through the power of his reasoning and logic, denies the possibility of any other genuine inner experience from the same event, there can be no harmony or love – either inwardly in relationship to oneself or outwardly in relationship with others.

The test of religious practice is finding a way to work with this diverging array of inner experiences in a loving manner. It most definitely requires a sense of humour and a degree of openness to the many paradoxes of daily human life.

Yet it is not easy to hold and work with paradox in our mind without becoming crippled by confusion. It feels messy and complicated and our inner chatter longs to clear and tidy things up into some sort of cohesive order. When this happens it is just another chance to practice right mindfulness and to let the chatter blow itself out.

Rising above the Whole State of the Present Life

These teachings[3], which are the traditional wisdom of all peoples in all parts of the world, have become virtually incomprehensible to modern man, although he, too, desires nothing more than somehow to be able to rise above 'the whole state of the present life.' He hopes to do so by growing rich, by moving around at ever-increasing speed, by travelling to the moon and into space.

Schumacher, A Guide for the Perplexed, p.13.

We have been exploring how to rise above the whole state of the present life, and to achieve greater happiness, by developing our inner faculties and gaining knowledge of the highest things. This is the traditional wisdom of all peoples in all parts of the world that have become virtually incomprehensible to modern man.

Happiness for me is a process more than a state of attainment. It is not about dwelling in some heavenly place above and beyond the drama of everyday life but it is about the movement towards transcendence. The experience of happiness arises when the moment of grace descends upon me and offers me those few crumbs of comfort to keep on the path up the mountainside. Suddenly in the midst of ordinariness something happens to shift the experience to a different level. It is in the shift that the feeling of happiness occurs.

Yet this longing for happiness remains universal; even if our tastes have changed somewhat in modern times. Is the desire to grow rich in

[3] The teachings referred to in the text are from Saint Thomas Aquinas (1225-1274)

material things only a modern phenomena; or is it just that in modern times we have made this experience more tantalisingly possible? Wealth in our modern world can now be gained through endeavour and not solely through privilege and it offers an incentive for a man poor in money to rise above the whole state of his present life by becoming rich. Is this desire for betterment wrong? It is not fair to call it wrong but it may be fair to call this desire unwise. For outer circumstances change as quickly as the wind and as a poor man may quickly become rich; a rich man can as easily become poor again.

There is no freedom and lasting happiness to be gained from the things of the world and there are no guarantees that we will be able to rise above the whole state of the present life by doing so. For the poverty that exists in the present life is caused by the cavity that exists in our heart and not by the state of our bank balance.

So if happiness cannot be gained from achieving the betterment of our circumstances can it be gained by the chase? If, as I have said, happiness arises in the movement towards something greater then can the tantalising prospect or opportunity of betterment give us the same experience? What I am asking is whether there is happiness to be found in our endeavours? There can only be happiness in our endeavours if there is a feeling of inner peace and contentment in ourselves. If our endeavours are merely trying to cover over our own inner feelings of emptiness; if we are merely trying to keep busy so as not to face the cavity in our own hearts then there is surely no happiness to be found here either.

If we cannot find happiness by getting rich or through our busy-ness, can we find it through travelling and pushing back our frontiers? To some extent we can find happiness through this endeavour. Having travelled the world myself I definitely feel as if I have been blessed to have visited some of the most beautiful parts of our planet. Many of the crumbs of comfort I've received over the years have come when travelling as there is something about being on holiday somewhere new that opens me to the experience of grace. It can sometimes feel hard to open when we are stuck in our familiar environment and in our daily rhythm and grind. Travelling shifts our perspective and broadens our horizons and there are some places in nature that can leave us truly humbled.

But pushing back the frontiers on the horizontal plane are no match for pushing back the frontiers of the vertical plane. There is so much more depth and richness in exploring and gaining knowledge of the highest things in ourselves than in exploring and gaining knowledge of places in the world. It also feels so much more sustainable and meaningful to open myself to the experience of grace whenever and wherever I am without having to travel somewhere new.

In many respects this is one of the ultimate challenges we face as human beings. How can I find happiness and peace in the here and now? How can I bring more love into my daily life without changing my circumstances?

Our Omnipotence is Wearing Thin

But there have also been positive changes: Some people are no longer angry when told that restoration must come from within; the belief that everything is 'politics' and that radical rearrangements of the system will suffice to save civilisation is no longer held with the same fanaticism as it was held twenty-five years ago. Everywhere in the modern world there are experiments in new life-styles and Voluntary Simplicity; the arrogance of materialistic Scientism is in decline, and it is sometimes tolerated even in polite society to mention God.

Admittedly some of this change of mind stems initially not from spiritual insight but from materialistic fear aroused by the environmental crisis, the fuel crisis, the threat of a food crisis, and the indications of a coming health crisis. In the face of these – and many other – threats, most people still try to believe in the 'technological fix.' If we could develop fusion energy, they say, our fuel problems would be solved; if we would perfect the processes of turning oil into edible proteins, the world's food problem would be solved; and the development of new drugs would surely avert any threat of a health crisis...and so on.

All the same, faith in modern man's omnipotence is wearing thin. Even if all the 'new' problems were solved by technological fixes, the state of futility, disorder, and corruption would remain. It existed before the present crises became acute, and it will not go away by itself.

Schumacher, A Guide for the Perplexed, p.138.

One of the things we looked at together in the previous meditation was whether there is happiness to be found in our endeavours. Looking at the years that have passed since the Guide was written it is fair to say that there have been a lot of positive developments and there are more people today who are engaged in what we may call more noble endeavours than ever before.

There does seem to be a growing awareness that the faith in our omnipotence was surely misplaced and it is probably fair to say that this is because the materialistic fears that were present at the time the Guide was written have not disappeared but have exacerbated since. But what can be done about it?

Yet it is interesting, and rather strange to see, that in times of fear we turn towards the one who is provoking the fear in us. The abused wife is too afraid to leave her husband and likewise we are too afraid to leave, what we have already called, the modern experiment. In times of crisis we look to our scientists to give us the technological fix. In times of illness we look to our doctors to give us the cure. In times of financial crisis we look to the economists to work out a solution. In times of political corruption we look to politicians to reform the system. Yet it is in facing these moments of fear, and in drawing strength from them, that we will have to turn things around. One day the abused wife will have to stand up and walk out of that door without looking back.

But it feels like a big risk for us to take. Because we are very comfortable and safe with what is known to us and we feel very shaky in walking out of that door into an uncertain and unknown future. What will possibly happen to us and our civilisation if we leave behind the modern experiment?

So even those who are engaged in noble endeavours of reform need to ask themselves whether they are simply improving the conditions in the prison house to make it appear more attractive and homely and whether they too are afraid to walk out of the prison altogether. Can lasting happiness and peace of mind arise inside of us even if we do make our prison mirror our own inner beliefs of what is right and what is wrong? What is the difference between someone pursuing the ambition of materialistic success and becoming a million-pound banker and someone pursuing the ambition of a more caring approach to the environment and becoming a respected environmentalist and political lobbyist? Both ambitions are driven by self-interest. Both ambitions are driven by the desire to create a better system for ourselves...and possibly others. Is this desire wrong?

Not at all. I am not here to judge your actions and if you wish to pursue your desires by all means go ahead. But at least do so with the awareness of your own inner fears and the awareness that whether you succeed or not will in no way make you more or less happy and at peace. Does it make you angry to be told that restoration must come from within and not without? Does it make you angry to be told that when you are busy trying to create a more just, fairer and healthier world for yourself and others that you are neglecting the one thing you are here to be on this planet, which is to love? Are your noble endeavours really coming out of a state of inner peace and love? Do you still feel you have the right and the omnipotence to improve the living conditions for yourself and others?

If your actions are stemming from fear rather than love, fear of walking out of that prison house altogether, then what can you do about it? How can we possibly find the strength and courage to claim our freedom back and to take that walk into the glorious unknown? This requires us to take the path of acceptance and forgiveness for ourselves, and also for others, so that they no longer have a hold over our heart. It is a path that must be walked alone.

So can we begin by accepting and forgiving the 'system' that was created by our modern experiment...even with all its brokenness and failings? Can we say honestly to ourselves that even in the midst of all the crises it creates that the system will not hold tyranny over my heart and over my capacity and willingness to love? Can we stay committed to our religious practice of staying in contact with a higher state of presence in ourselves even in the midst of the drama?

Then out of this loving space we create for ourselves we become free to act and to bring about real and lasting transformation and change. For our actions will be clear and sharp and the shackles of fear that once inhibited us will have been thrown off for good.

The Real Difference

All the 'humanities,' as distinct from the natural sciences, deal in
one way or another with consciousness. But a distinction between
consciousness and self awareness is rarely drawn. As a result,
modern thinking has become increasingly uncertain whether or
not there is any 'real' difference between animal and man. A
great deal of study of the behaviour of animals is being
undertaken for the purpose of understanding the nature of man.
This is analogous to studying physics with the hope of learning
something about life. Naturally, since man, as it were, *contains*
the three lower Levels of Being, certain things about him can be
elucidated by studying minerals, plants, and animals – in fact,
everything can be learned about him *except that which makes
him human.*

Schumacher, A Guide for the Perplexed, p.20.

Let us turn back again now to the 'modern experiment' that we are
afraid to leave behind. What we are suffering with in ourselves is a loss of
empowerment and a lack of faith which inhibits us from walking out of
this prison house altogether. Why do we abandon ourselves and why do
we deny our own inner voice of wisdom, which if we listened to it
carefully, would tell us to leave?

It is time to explore why we choose to live in limitation. There is a
story of a frog who spent his life living in a well, and who, upon stepping
out of his well and seeing the vastness of the ocean, found his mind

exploding. We too simply cannot comprehend the possibilities and opportunities that are afforded to us as human beings and we choose to stay in a place of limitation which we know so well. Yet is it really a problem if we are content in this place and choose not to step out and realise our full potential. Unfortunately our planet is crying out for human beings to step fully into their power and to assume their rightful place in the great circle of life. The time for transformation has come.

There is a similar tale that is told in the Disney classic The Lion King. Having been chased away from his pride by his evil uncle after the death of his father, Simba grows up denying who he really is and instead chooses to 'hang out' with two 'lower' animals in the kingdom. He eventually remembers and awakens to the truth of who he really is and returns back to assume his rightful place in the circle of life. In doing so the health and vitality of the ecosystem is restored and order is returned to the kingdom.

What is interesting about this classic archetypal story is the absence of initiation. After the sudden death of his father Simba had lost the elder figure who could teach him the ways of wise kingship. The two 'lower' animals he befriended could only initiate him into their 'lesser' way of life and his potential was left unfulfilled.

We too are crying out for wise elders who can help us to remember and to awaken to the fullness of who we are as human beings. Unfortunately we find ourselves with 'lower' animals as our teachers and these are the ones who are very effective at studying the properties of minerals and plants, and the behaviour of animals, in the hope of understanding the nature of man. What are we to do when learned professionals tell us, with good intentions, to take a dose of medicine because it worked effectively on a laboratory rat?

So who do we turn to for advice and wisdom if not to our teachers? How can we possibly begin to remember and awaken to the fullness of who we are as human beings in such a deserted environment and wasteland?

These pose challenging questions about destiny and faith. In the Lion King it was destined in the storyline that Simba would eventually awaken and that an experience of grace would descend upon him from the heavens to trigger this awakening. We too have a storyline that is unfolding as we move through our lives. This is our soul's journey of awakening that underlies everything that happens on the surface of our lives. At some point in our soul's storyline the moment will come when grace will descend upon us and transform our lives completely. It is all a question of timing and of being open and faithful to the possibility of the graced event.

So although we may be in a deserted environment and wasteland, having learned everything about ourselves except that which makes us truly human, we can still anticipate and set our eyes upon the green shoot that may suddenly burst through out of nowhere. When that shoot bursts forth we will have that opportunity to leave our prison behind forever and we will finally know deep in our hearts the real difference between a stone, a plant, an animal and a man.

The Backbone of Descriptive Science

If we look carefully at what the various sciences...actually do, we find that we can divide them roughly into two groups; those which are primarily *descriptive* of what can actually be seen or otherwise experienced and those which are primarily *instructional* of how certain systems work and be made to produce predictable results...The difference between these two groups is seldom observed, with the result that most philosophies of science, in fact, are found to relate only to the instructional sciences and treat the descriptive ones as nonexisting. It is not, as has often been asserted, as if the difference between 'descriptive' and 'instructional' signified merely degrees of maturity or stages in the development of a science.

Schumacher, A Guide for the Perplexed, p.103.

Through this meditation we are starting to look more deeply at what is taught to us by 'lower' animals so as to get more of a sense of the fact that their level of understanding is missing a beat somehow. It is like listening to an orchestra playing and being told, quite correctly, by the teacher next to you which instruments are the ones producing the different sounds. Yet if this is all we take from our experience of the orchestra then we are missing a beat because we never hear the symphony and we miss the truth that the whole is much bigger than the sum of all the parts.

In this instance, instructional science is, as we have already looked at, very effective at dealing with the mineral kingdom. These are the sciences of mathematics, chemistry and physics which have done tremendous work in helping us to understand the laws of this kingdom. It has made such progress because of this thing we call time. It is through time that scientists have been able to experiment, and gradually, by process of deduction and elimination, have been getting clearer and clearer. It is like trying to bake a cake. At first you might put in some rough estimation in the measurement of ingredients and in the time and temperature you need to bake it. Then as you bake that cake more and more times over the years you hone ever more finely an exact and precise calculation. Instructional sciences are most suited to this task and it is indeed their purpose to get more exact and precise in their instructions.

So there is no need to apply *blame* to our scientists simply because their instructions cannot be applied to the other, higher, kingdoms. We need not become frustrated when their instructions do not help us understand what it means to be a living, conscious, self aware human being in the world. The 'lower' animals are teaching us what they know, and their knowledge has its place in the circle of life. Knowledge of chemical and mathematical laws is highly valuable for certain practical purposes.

Yet we need to be wary when the 'lower' animals say to us that they will be able to provide us with these 'higher' answers if we give them more time so that their science can develop and mature. It is in saying this that the instructive sciences descend from science for understanding to science for manipulation.

What are needed to keep our instructional sciences in check are descriptive sciences – namely life sciences, social sciences and so-called humanities – that have more backbone to them. The weak backbone arises from the fear that because they cannot draw conclusions that their descriptions are not valid. Where does this fear stem from? There seems to be an underlying belief here that man, through the power of his intelligence alone, can know the mind of God. Is there an expectation here that we should be able to know and to give instructions on how to create life from no-life? Is there an expectation here that we should be able to know and to give instructions on how to create consciousness from no-consciousness? Is there an expectation here that we should be able to know and to give instructions on how to create self-awareness from no-self-awareness? It is because we have these expectations that we do not value what the descriptive sciences can observe and describe from the appearance of life, consciousness and self-awareness. We think they need to be able to provide more information of what is going in these kingdoms before they can be recognised as valid and legitimate. In the meantime they are treated as undeveloped.

It reflects a problem that we too face in ourselves as human beings. We too desire validity and legitimacy for who we are as individuals and in doing so we often strive for little trophies to prove our worth. It seems to be a common problem for many that we lack the sense of inner self worth that gives us the peace of mind to take our rightful place in the whole. We think we need to be doing more and pushing back our frontiers in order to 'develop' ourselves and to gain the respect and sense of worth from others. We try and mould ourselves to fit in with other people's expectations and it is not enough to simply be who we truly are. In lacking that sense of inner self worth we have no backbone.

The descriptive sciences try and do the same things that we do as human beings. They try and portray an image of validity and legitimacy and in doing so they descend into the realm of science for manipulation rather than genuine science for understanding. It is the descriptive sciences themselves that do not wish to be distinct from the instructional sciences because they lack the self worth to go it alone.

The relationship between the instructional and descriptive sciences perhaps best serves as a metaphor to help us to develop our own backbone and inner self worth so that we ourselves are not swayed by the forces of manipulation. It is in staying true to ourselves that we can live with integrity and wisdom; even if that means taking a path that receives no outside approval or assistance from our peers.

<u>The Eye of the Heart</u>

The power of 'the Eye of the Heart,' which produces *insight*, is vastly superior to the power of thought, which produces *opinions*.

Schumacher, A Guide for the Perplexed, p.47.

Having considered that our backbone needs to be strengthened through the development of inner self worth, we now move back again to the question and matter of faith.

For the paradox is that we cannot guarantee positive results and there is no certainty that having taken the plunge to go it alone that we will be rewarded for our courage. Not instantly anyway. But this is what we really want is it not? We are a society that has got used to instant gratification and expect things to happen immediately. We are a society that craves the reassurance of visible results for our efforts; and if we don't receive this at the click of our fingers then doubts begin to arise. Our faith it seems has been planted in a bed of sand.

So how do we overcome this and cultivate faith in our own inner wisdom? How do we live our lives with complete integrity to the insights and intuitions we receive? How do we *know* that the power of the 'Eye of the Heart' is vastly superior to the power of thought?

The leap of faith we must make will probably not arise overnight. There is likely to be a dance that we make in stepping forward and stepping back over many years. For some this dance may go on for more than one lifetime. It seems that for many of us there is a learning process that unfolds as we dabble with the Eye of the Heart and its powers and

47

lessen our reliance on the power of thought.

This takes us into the field of spiritual practice for it is in this that we take the time out of our daily lives and to explore and contemplate our own inner landscape. Through our spiritual practice we begin to know ourselves more intimately and to discover for ourselves whether there is the Eye of the Heart that exists inside of us.

So in the beginning we have to stop and step outside the maelstrom of our daily lives. We have to open ourselves to the possibility that there is a different world that we can experience beyond the world we create with the power of our thought. In many respects this can be a leap of faith in itself and we often need some spark to initiate this action of turning around and stepping back. Sometimes it can be a moment of sheer beauty and grace that shakes us, but more often than not, it is a moment of pain and suffering that causes us to stop. Sometimes our body finds mischievous ways of developing symptoms to tell us to slow down and take stock.

Having created some space for ourselves we can begin to consider the inner world that lies beyond the thinking mind. As we have explored together before; the thinking mind is nothing other than the part of us which needs to create a story in order to make sense and bring order to the jumble of our experiences. It is the noisy constant chatter of our own ego mind which is constantly producing a stream of opinions and judgments about what we are doing. It is the part of us that dwells in time and can never rest in loving acceptance of what truly is in this present moment. But in the space around this we can allow the Eye of the Heart in ourselves to emerge. Indeed, it is only in this place of stillness and acceptance deep inside that genuine acts of creativity can arise.

Yet, as has been said, there is no guarantee that insights will suddenly arise once we go beyond the thinking mind. There is no guarantee that we will see and experience the full power that can be expressed through the Eye of the Heart. For we are not in control here and can only water the soil in the trust that something will grow. But it is through the dedication to our spiritual practice that we prepare the soil, plant the seeds, and tend lovingly to our little plot. Then maybe one day grace will descend and we will suddenly see something start to shoot through into life. The dance pulls us in and we feel that we are beginning to see. Then before we know it something happens to cause that shoot to wilt and we pull back again from the dance in doubt. But the next time grace descends we are a little more prepared for it and its root into the soil goes down that little bit more deeply. And so the dance continues.

Eventually we will get to the point of surrender and to the place where there is no separation between us and the object of our dance. We have become one with the dance and the power of thought no longer holds us in its grasp. Now we finally *know* that the power of the Eye of the Heart is vastly superior and we can act with firm courage on the insights we receive.

Unity of Knowledge

The unity of knowledge is destroyed when one or several of the Four Fields of Knowledge[4] remain uncultivated, and also when a field is cultivated with instruments and methodologies which are appropriate only in quite another field.

Schumacher, A Guide for the Perplexed, p.118.

So far in our meditations we have been largely considering together the Fourth Field of Knowledge which allows us to address the question of what I actually observe in the world around me. As we have already considered, the instructional sciences are most suited to this task and we need to develop our descriptive sciences to provide a stronger backbone alongside them. It is this backbone that allows our descriptive sciences to act as a bridge between this field of knowledge and the other three fields.

And as we have already explored together, ultimately it is us ourselves that need to develop a strong enough backbone so that we can move into all the four fields and to achieve the unity of knowledge that we need to live in this world as a mature human being. Yet as we have also considered, we have no teachers that are clearly available to us and

---

[4] "The four questions which lead to these fields of knowledge may be put like this: 1) What is really going on in my own inner world? 2) What is really going on in the inner world of other beings? 3) What do I look like in the eyes of other beings? 4) What do I actually observe in the world around me?" (Schumacher, A Guide for the Perplexed, p.62-63).

who can give us our education.

What we have at our disposal from our education is a half-empty toolbox with tools that are not suitable to the task. We have acquired great intelligence about the world and how it operates and each of us individually can choose to specialise in one or more of these areas if we so desire...or we can simply let others do the thinking for us. It is, when we think about it, quite incredible what technology has given to us and what is normal and accepted by us today would have seemed incomprehensible to our ancestors not so long ago.

Yet our obsession with conquering the world through our intelligence has not brought us any lasting comfort or satisfaction. On the material level many of us today live in conditions that only the very privileged would have enjoyed a century ago and yet deep down we are no happier or at ease with ourselves than any other generation.

It has been said that we are reaching the age of relationship because no longer do we have to spend our days dealing with our separate and individual economic circumstances. If we look to our ancestors we can see how much time and energy they had to put in each day just to meet their most basic needs of food and shelter. Their endeavours over the centuries have ensured that today we only truly need to spend a small, very tiny proportion, of our time to meet our most basic needs. The economic problem has been solved for all of us.

Yet despite this we continue to work long hours and we try and convince ourselves that there are still economic problems that need to be addressed. We are perhaps not quite ready to believe and accept that this is completely unnecessary. We are perhaps not quite ready to stop our busy lives and we are perhaps not quite ready to know what to do with our time if we are not out there doing a 'job' like everyone else.

The reason why we are not ready is because our toolbox is half-empty. If we had the tools would we not feel it was more valuable to devote our time to learning and developing through the other three fields of knowledge than continuing to busy ourselves by making up and solving problems in the fourth field of knowledge? It is as if we have only a screwdriver in our toolbox and even though there are some loose nails that need hammering on the object we are working on, we choose to keep unscrewing and screwing a single screw in the corner because this is the only tool we have in our hand. Yet it is when we finally stop and see the insanity of this and to begin to make a hammer for ourselves that we discover that our time is being spent much more valuably than ever before.

Ours is the age of relationship because the other three fields of knowledge are all to do with relationship – both the relationship with ourselves and with others. It is through our relationships that we can develop our skills in the other fields of knowledge and to achieve the unity of the four fields that we need.

The instrument we have at our disposal to cultivate relationships is love. However, although love is fully present in our hearts right now it is the hardest job we can do to remove the armour that we put around it. It is because it is so hard to do that we choose to keep ourselves busy doing a hundred other jobs that are truly less important and we deny that the other three fields of knowledge even exist.

As long as we stubbornly hold on to these old habits there can be no true relationship because there can be no love. Our interactions with ourselves and others become a ground for conflict rather than a ground for peace and harmony. The drama of conflict that we create for ourselves goes right back to the beginning of man. It is the human story that we have been retelling ourselves over and over. But are you now ready to change the script?

On Life

The extraordinary thing about the modern 'life sciences' is that they hardly ever deal with *life as such*...but devote infinite attention to the study and analysis of the physiochemical body that is life's carrier. It may well be that modern science has no method for coming to grips with *life as such*. If this is so, let it be frankly admitted; there is no excuse for the pretense that life is nothing but physics and chemistry.

Schumacher, A Guide for the Perplexed, p.19.

Let us turn together now to look and deal with *life as such*. In this I mean looking at it in ourselves and exploring the question of what is this life that exists inside of me? We may say that we know we are alive because we are breathing or we may get a sense of life when its force is diminished inside of us. Some days we just feel a little bit flatter as if our life force has been drained and we are slightly off colour. Of course physics and chemistry may be able to observe and provide a description of what is going on in our body during the different moods we go through and can show us exactly the effect that a diminishment in life force has on the chemistry of the brain. But what it cannot show us is the location of the on-off switch.

Why is it important for us as individuals to look and deal with this question rather than simply leave it to the scientists to explore? It is important because it can be a humbling experience to know how rare, precious and vulnerable this thing is within us. Often we need to have a close and sudden experience of death before we begin to appreciate the value and gift of life. How does the appreciation of life change our perspective on things?

For what we observe of those who've had the close encounter with death and are still alive, is that they tend to live with a greater sense of humility, awe and respect in their experiences in this world. The omnipotence they felt before has been shattered and they are no longer in the control tower at the centre of their universe. It also helps shift perspective towards the things that are truly important and often leads to a reprioritisation of how one's time is spent. Suddenly things that once seemed important now seem to be hollow and empty pursuits. Often this reprioritisation leads people to realise the value of healthy relationships in their life and ends the chase for other goals that come at the expense of those closest to them. They are no longer interested in getting that one step ahead in the competitive race.

A close encounter with death also helps give us a glimpse of a world that exists beyond the illusory world of form. We see the fleetingness of the things of the world and start to see the real essence and nature beyond them. It opens us up to the experience of grace and God. We start to become more interested in questions of meaning and purpose and no longer do we meekly accept when we are told that we are nothing more than a cog in the machine that needs to keep on turning and turning.

All these things are denied to us as we simply nod our heads when told that life is nothing but physics and chemistry. All these things are denied to us when we go through our lives without acknowledging and making friends with the grim reaper who is always there with us on our shoulder. Why do we need to have to go through the shock treatment before we listen to his wisdom? Why do we need to go through severe health problems, a near-death experience, or the experience of sudden loss of a close friend or family member before things start to turn around? Why are we unable to choose for ourselves a healthy relationship with life and death from a position of strength?

Let us ask ourselves again why the pretence that life is nothing but physics and chemistry denies us the possibility of this healthy relationship? For a start it tells us that these matters are best left to the experts. We turn the matter over to our doctors to take care of our lives rather than taking on the responsibility ourselves. In doing so we seem to think that we can pollute our minds and bodies as much as we want without having to face the consequences because the doctor will be on hand to give us a magic pill that keeps our motor ticking over. We also don't learn and grow through our experiences because we try to convince ourselves that we are immortal and are our own masters of time. We think that there is always tomorrow to make amends.

But what would happen if our experts turned around tomorrow and confessed to us that they can't get to grips with life as such and that we will have to find our own way to get to grips with it? What would happen if our doctors started to hesitate before prescribing us drugs because they openly said to us that they didn't really know what was going on to cause the diminishment of life force within us? Suddenly without this safety net we would be brought face to face with our own mortality. The whisperings of the grim reaper in our own ear would start to get a little louder and we would need to begin taking responsibility for this thing we call life ourselves.

Loving your Neighbour

To be able to take the inner life of my neighbor seriously, it is necessary that I take my own inner life seriously. But what does that mean? It means that I must put myself in a condition where I can truly observe what is going on and begin to understand what I observe. In modern times there is no lack of understanding of the fact that man is a *social* being...Hence there is no lack of exhortation that he should love his neighbor – or at least not be nasty to him – and should treat him with tolerance, compassion and understanding. At the same time, however, the cultivation of self-knowledge has fallen into virtually total neglect, except, that is, where it is the object of active suppression. That you cannot love your neighbor unless you love yourself; that you cannot understand your neighbor unless you understand yourself; that there can be no knowledge of the 'invisible person' who is your neighbor except on the basis of self knowledge – these fundamental truths have been forgotten even by many of the professionals in the established religions.

Schumacher, A Guide for the Perplexed, p.84.

This is one of the most powerful quotes we will be exploring together in this book and in many respects this is what I am practicing in order to try and understand the heart and essence of Fritz's teaching. As I confessed in the introduction I did not know Fritz personally but I have been trying to get to know and understand him by getting to know and understand myself. This is one of the most powerful teachings that we would be wise to explore together.

One of the main reasons why there is such an intolerable level of discord in our relationships with others is because of our lack of self-awareness and self-knowledge. It is as if our own ego mind, which has been left to rule the roost, gets in between ourselves and our neighbour (and probably their ego mind too). In effect there is very rarely a genuine interaction of two beings but instead we have many interactions of two egos. Now let us remind ourselves that our ego mind is busy trying to create order out of the jumble of our experiences. It is the part of us that tries to box and file things away in accordance with our beliefs about how the world is. If our neighbour says something to us we do not hear what he or she is trying to express directly but only get a sense of it once it has gone through our own interior sorting office. This is why we have so many religions, and so many factions within our religions, because we read the same religious text and interpret it in completely different ways. Not only do we interpret it in different ways but we go to war over it (and usually in spite of our exhortations of tolerance and compassion). In doing so we miss the heart and essence of what the text is trying to teach us and we destroy the possibility of relationship.

So it is through the cultivation of self-awareness and self-knowledge that we get a sense of how our sorting office works and we become more wary of what comes to us at the other end. Instead we start to look at ways to bypass our sorting office altogether and to meet our neighbour on a heart-to-heart level. Through our practice we begin to see how our own self-interest manipulates the interactions we have and we see the ways in which we judge others based on our own theories and assumptions about who they are and what they are up to.

Is there any value in keeping the sorting office open? In looking at it we can perhaps see that we built it in the first place to provide a defence mechanism that protected the organism from attack. We shield our hearts from others because we don't always know where our neighbour is coming from. It is part of our animal instinct that we have inherited and it is the way in which we use our five senses to get a lie of the land. If our neighbour is speaking or acting harshly then, even if the words or actions are not directed against us, we still do not want our neighbour's energy to pierce through to our soft spot. Our sorting office helps us to guess, based on our limited understanding, whether the information coming through our senses is safe or not.

This is the habitual reflexive behaviour that goes on inside of us. Yet what we are trying to cultivate through self-awareness is the recognition that these perceived threats to our heart are merely an illusion. Fear has to give way to love and defensiveness has to give way to openness. For as we grow in self-awareness we begin to see that this is the edge we have to cross in order to fulfil our potential as human beings. We need to extend ourselves beyond our own separated boundary of self-interest and step into the universal state of oneness and wholeness. Qualities of courage, faith and trust must be carefully cultivated as we come to know the truth that one's essence cannot be destroyed by outside forces because there is, in truth, no separation that exists between self and other. If there is love within then so will there be love without. Our heart is one with the heart of God and of all life. In recent times we can look to the life story of Mahatma Gandhi as a human being who realised this profound truth. He is one person who shows to us the transformation of fear into love. He is a person who understood that you cannot love and understand your neighbour unless you first love and understand yourself.

So what happens when you meet your neighbour from a place beyond your ego mind and with an open heart? If the other is open to it there is the possibility that love and grace will arise in the relationship as well as this precious gift of mutual understanding through the meeting of minds.

What happens when you read A Guide for the Perplexed, or some other sacred text, in the same way? There is the possibility that you will hear what the writer was really trying to communicate from beyond the limited range of words that he or she has to convey their teaching. Instead of trying to bring *down* the teaching to our level of understanding we instead are lifted *up* to theirs.

On Proof

With the light of the intellect we can see things which are invisible to our bodily senses. No one denies that mathematical and geometrical truths are 'seen' in this way. To *prove* a proposition means to give it form, by analysis, simplification, transformation, or dissection, through which the truth can be seen; beyond this seeing there is neither the possibility of nor the need for any further proof.

Schumacher, A Guide for the Perplexed, p.46.

This meditation leads us to consider one of the strange paradoxes. We have talked at length about the instructional sciences and how they endeavour over time to get closer and closer to a full understanding of how the *mineral kingdom* functions. This may lead us to a perception of scientists being very cold and rational in their calculations as they deduce and hone in on a more accurate picture. Yet if we add in the human factor we get a completely different perception of how the process of discovering new truths actually happens. It seems as if the breakthrough experience really does not arise in this way. It reminds me of a documentary that I watched many years ago of one eminent mathematician who described the process of discovering new mathematical truths as a peak experience which arose from a completely different part of his consciousness. The breakthrough experience came out of his intuition and any new and significant discoveries must indeed come from this place. It requires the human being, who is seeing the new truth, to have taken a leap of faith in believing that there was something new to be discovered over the horizon. It requires the human being to employ the light of his intellect in order to go beyond the known.

So what we are implying here is that even though the instructional sciences dismiss the significance of the human factor in one sense; they are busily proving it in another. In their daily work they are actually showing that there has to be more going on than the workings of a detached ego mind that is busily ordering and making sense of data that comes through our bodily senses. Although there is *intelligence* to be found in this sorting process it is not the *full light of the intellect* to which we are referring here. Truth cannot be seen and discovered through the sorting process alone...although, strangely, it is also the case that truth cannot be seen without the sorting process either.

We need to prepare the ground so that the form of our lives has some coherence and order to it. We need to learn how to live healthily in ego consciousness. In science we need the training and discipline in our field of study to be able to analyse, simplify, transform and dissect the object we are studying.

Yet although we may get our house in order, it does not guarantee for us that we will see the truth or have the peak experience that takes us to a different state of consciousness. The moment of grace is in truth as likely to descend on the one whose life is undisciplined and chaotic as the one who has brought their life into perfect order. The light of the intellect is there inside all of us regardless of whether we pay attention to it or not and whether we prepare the ground for it to shine through or not.

This appears paradoxical but in truth it is about keeping us from the extremes of black or white. If we become too obsessed and absorbed with discipline and coherence then we are encouraged to loosen and lighten and to remember not to take our ego mind too seriously. If we are too undisciplined and scattered in our lives then we are encouraged to bring some order back to our lives by developing through our ego mind.

In truth, however, we can only really begin to recognise our peak experiences when we have reached a healthy place in ego consciousness.

We need to take our ego mind to its very limits so we can know and recognise when we have an experience that simply cannot be explained by our ego mind. When this happens we will know that we have entered sacred ground and that something significant is happening to us. We will be more alive to the moment when grace descends and will be less likely to let it slip by unnoticed.

It is the moment when we climb above the clouds and breathe in the clearer air that we know we haven't tasted before. Then whatever insights we receive in this state of mind will be recognised with absolute certainty and the seer will know that there truly isn't a need for any further proof of what has come to them. They have had the flash of understanding which has taken them beyond what was previously grasped by their ego mind. And although others may clearly see the new truth that is being communicated to them; they will not be able to fathom where that jewel emerged from. It will appear as if it has come from nowhere.

A Strange Country

In this life we find ourselves as in a strange country...Decisions have to be taken that we are not ready for; aims have to be chosen that we cannot see clearly. This is very strange and on the face of it, quite irrational. Human beings, it seems, are insufficiently 'programmed.' Not only are they utterly helpless when they are born and remain so for a long time; even when fully grown, they do not move and act with the sure-footedness of animals. They hesitate, doubt, change their minds, run hither and thither, uncertain not simply of how to get what they want but above all of *what* they want.

Schumacher, A Guide for the Perplexed, p.6.

What do I really want and why is it that answering this question feels so difficult a lot of the time? I sense that the real reason is the element of choice and free will that I have at my fingertips. Sometimes it feels as if there is too much choice and too many decisions to make and I wonder whether our so-called free market which offers to us these choices is a good thing. Is it not easier just to act on our instincts like other animals do and to regain our sure-footedness?

Yet we are often told that the layer of complexity we have created for ourselves through our economic situation is a good thing. Choice and competition in the marketplace is designed to improve standards and to create better value for money. But is it not true that it can only be a good thing if we take out the human factor altogether? For the free market can only run smoothly and perfectly if human beings themselves conform to some image of perfection and rationalism. Yet it seems as if we have been inadequately programmed to cope with the volume of choices at our disposal. The ego mind that is responsible for sorting through the information and making sense of it all is overwhelmed by the amount of information it is being asked to process. Then things get a little cloudy for us as we struggle to cope and we struggle to wade through.

It is interesting that we were expected to develop our ego minds at the same pace as we were developing our economy. It was not enough for us to live within the confines of our raw bodily instinct that was solely concerned with survival. We wanted to stretch ourselves and to thrive by gaining mastery of our environment. Yet gaining mastery over the environment becomes a never ending chase and new layers of complexity keep forming as we do so. Those whose minds simply couldn't keep up with the chase were left behind to look on forlornly and with bemusement at the new world they found themselves in. Just imagine someone from the 19th century suddenly appearing in our 21st century lives and imagine the shock they would have in what they saw. I doubt their mind would be able to cope or make any sense of the world they found themselves in and probably wouldn't be able to recognise it as the same world that they once inhabited. If we ever take a moment to stop and to take a step back then we too would be quite shocked by the world we live in. Things that were considered flights of fantasy a few generations ago are just part of normal everyday living for us today. Telephones, motor vehicles, aeroplanes, computers, the internet, mobile telephones, and all other technologies which have come our way. The pace of daily life is speeding up before our eyes and we are warned to keep up or face the consequences.

But most of us do seem to be able to cope and to just about keep up with the chase; albeit a little breathlessly. Although we haven't been programmed to perform as the highly efficient processing machines that our world requires us to be; we do a good job in pretending. In doing so though we are building up a backlog of stuff that hasn't been dealt with properly. Sometimes we may come right to the end of our lives before we are hit with all that has been left behind in the chase or we may develop bodily symptoms from the stress we put ourselves under.

Often it is our relationships with others that suffer from the chase because we spend our lives constantly 'in our heads' sorting through and processing all these choices and decisions that need to be made. Yet it is only when we stop and learn to dwell in that place beyond our ego minds that true relationship emerges because it is only here that we learn what love is. In stopping it isn't about regressing back to the place where we live solely on our instincts or where we try and plead with someone else to do everything for us. It isn't about having a preference for a communist arrangement over the free market.

So choices will need to be made and our free will continually exercised. Yet choices have to be handled in a different way. To begin with we need to first accept that we will never achieve the gold prize by becoming fully programmed in order to cope effortlessly with anything that life throws at us. We will never be that super efficient processing machine that can move sure-footedly in the world and that has complete mastery over it. No matter how hard we strive for it, and no matter how many people teach us how to strive for it, we will always fail. From this hopeless place of surrender we can then start to learn how to dwell in the magical place of not-knowing and of not having everything all figured out. We will learn to live and thrive in the uncertainty of the moment where we do not know what it is that we do want.

From this uncertainty something unexpected may descend, namely, an intuitive moment of clarity and inspiration that comes to guide us onwards to our next step and beyond.

A World of Ideas

Here it is necessary simply to recognize that sense data alone do not produce insight or understanding of any kind. *Ideas* produce insight and understanding and the world of ideas lie within us.

Schumacher, A Guide for the Perplexed, p.48.

In these meditations it feels as if we are returning again and again to the recognition that sense data alone do not produce insight or understanding of any kind. What is there that is left for us to explore together from this recognition? What are we missing that is causing us to return back to this theme again and again?

Let us look at the last phrase of this quote; the world of ideas lie within us. It feels as if there is something new that is being spoken of here. For what is the distinction between an idea and an opinion?

We know that opinions are formed out of our interpretation of sense data. We are constantly forming opinions about the world and the people around us as we go through our daily lives. But is this different from forming *ideas* about the world and the people around us? Where do our ideas come from if not from our observations?

One distinction between an idea and an opinion is that opinions are formed when we register the outer differences between existing things whereas ideas are formed when we get a sense of the inner meaning behind the appearance. It is as if ideas come to us when there is a sudden illumination of the invisible from behind the visible. Ideas are formed when we learn to read between the lines of what people say and receive an impression of what the person is really trying to convey.

But if this capacity to produce ideas is within us; where does it come from? What is the force or mechanism that allows us to see the invisible from behind the visible? To understand this requires a shift from a materialist perspective of the universe to a spiritual perspective. Whereas a material perspective only allows us to see the world of matter, a spiritual perspective opens us up to a world of energy. In the language of science we descend down into the quantum world which tells us that the world of matter is merely an illusion and that once you look deeper all you see is empty space. In this empty space we have an ever shifting energy field and it is in this energy field that ideas are formed. It is as if we can go beyond the sense of separateness that exists between me and you and to connect more deeply at this level. Rather than forming opinions about you I can instead get a more intimate and accurate idea of truth. It is in this field that I can come to know myself and to know God.

So the force is within us but it is not personal to us. It is like saying that God is within us but is bigger and vaster than us. This is a difficult one for our little minds to grasp for such a perspective does not sit comfortably and is not easy to comprehend.

We have already spoken about 'the Eye of the Heart' which is the force inside of us that allows us to tap into this field. It is where we get intuitive hunches not only about the people around us in space but also of our next steps in time. We get a feel for what is really going on and we start to live our lives more from a place of attunement as we learn to connect with the field more consciously. Instead of exhausting ourselves by acting and reacting to the surface details we begin to act with more precision and incisiveness as we see more clearly what needs to be done next. We have the clairvoyance to know exactly what is best in each situation we find ourselves in and our habitual myopia and narrow self-interest is put to bed. Through this we regain our sense of sure-footedness and poise as we choose to go beyond the vast gorge of opinions that are being formed in our minds and which creates such a world of problems for ourselves and others.

Does such a world sound phantasmagorical to you? Can you

imagine living a life solely from your ideas about the situation rather than from your opinions? Yet whether you think it is impossible or not; the force is there inside of you and it only needs your faith to activate it.

Those Very Special Mirrors

Everybody has a natural curiosity as to what he looks like, what
he sounds like, and what impression he makes on others. But the
'very special mirrors'...do not exist on this earth, perhaps merci-
fully so. The shocks they would administer might be more than
we could take. It is always painful to realise that there really is
quite a lot wrong with oneself, and we possess many mechanisms
to protect ourselves from this revelation. Our natural curiosity,
therefore does not take us very far...and we are all too easily
diverted into studying the faults of others rather than our own.

Schumacher, A Guide for the Perplexed, p.96.

In the previous meditation we spoke about ideas being formed
when there is an illumination of the invisible from behind the visible. Yet
it is not only ideas about other people that need to be formed as we
connect with the universal energy field; we also need to form ideas about
ourselves.

It is true that we can easily turn inwards and illuminate for ourselves as to what is going on inside of us. We can easily form impressions
about ourselves and what we are doing. These may or may not be truthful as it depends on how well we know our own inner landscape and to
what extent we have gained mastery over the musings of our ego mind.

Yet what we cannot illuminate easily is how other people see us.
Why is this important if we are capable of turning inward ourselves? Why
do I need to know how I appear to the world when these appearances are

merely an illusion and can never capture the essence of who I am? As long as I know that I am loving and wise, does it really matter what others think of me?

This knowledge is important because it helps to cultivate a healthy dose of *humility* in our lives. It pricks our sense of self importance and takes away the feeling that the world revolves around us and that we are at the centre of the universe. These are feelings that can arise if we happen to become too self absorbed into our own little world where we are safe, protected, and in control.

So it seems as if we don't really want to take responsibility for what we are putting out there into the world. We may convince ourselves that we are decent, loving individuals and we may put the blame on the other whenever we lose our poise. It feels too heavy a burden to always bring things back to oneself and to look at how we are creating whatever difficult situation we find ourselves in…or looking at what we need to learn by being here in this uncomfortable place.

There is clearly a difficult balance that needs to be sought here. Self-flagellation is not a healthy or loving way of responding to our own faults and we need to find a way of becoming self-aware in a tender and caring manner. Like a mother nurturing a child through the many mistakes that he or she will make as they grow up, we too have to nurture ourselves through our mistakes and through the many ways that we will miss the mark in what we say or do. Whilst it is never suitable for the mother to be abusive to her child, it is also not healthy for the mother to fuel the precociousness of the child by puffing up the child's sense of self importance. If she consistently says that there is nothing wrong with her little angel then that child will most certainly grow up as a terror inflicting all sorts of harm on themselves and others.

So we need to be careful when we are tuning in and forming ideas about our situation and the people around us that we are not excluding ourselves from the equation. If this happens then our ideas will not be truthful and we will be back in that place of forming opinions and conclusions that are not fully accurate. We need to remember that we are a part of the whole picture here and cannot separate ourselves from it. We are both the observer of the situation and the observed in the situation.

This is tricky for us to grasp because we inherently feel distinct from the other person or from the situation. We are here and the other person is there. If the other person is angry and upset we look solely at what is within the field of the other person to have caused this turmoil without wishing to recognise that we too are in the field.

Yet lasting relationships are forged when the two individuals involved are *willing* and committed in looking into the special mirrors that illuminate whether there is any hypocrisy in them too. Do your relationships have this quality of willingness or do you take the easy way out by keeping yourself separate from the world you live in and from its madness that you observe?

The Refining of Science

It is highly significant that as descriptive science becomes more refined and accurate, the rash utilitarian-materialistic doctrines of the nineteenth century are crumbling away one by one.

Schumacher, A Guide for the Perplexed. p.117.

We explored together in an earlier meditation the rather gloomy perspective that our descriptive sciences have lacked the backbone to stand up to the false philosophy of the instructional sciences, and have as a consequence lost their integrity as they try and make themselves appear to be more valid in the eyes of science.

Yet there are rays of light being shone by some individuals working in the field and it is important to recognise that the gloominess is not all pervasive. It is not only those working in the descriptive sciences who are challenging the rash utilitarian-materialistic doctrines but there are some physicists and chemists who are being humbled by the realisation that there are a lot of things about the world that remain a mystery to them. And it is not as if these are unimportant details at the fringes that they haven't quite got around to looking at. Instead they are beginning to realise that there are certain laws that are fundamental to the way the world works that they simply do not have a clue about. I sense that it is a massive step for an eminent physicist or chemist to take in admitting to themselves and their peers that their science simply cannot grasp or make sense of the mysteries of life, consciousness and self-awareness. But that step is being taken by some courageous individuals which will be for

71

the betterment of science. These scientists are creating space for those working in the descriptive fields to step in and to fill the void. Of course they can only go so far in describing what is being observed but at least their refined and accurate observations can act as fuel for inquiry.

It is through the accurate work of the descriptive sciences that we will once again become curious about the things that religion once taught us in order to fill the void.

How very strange that life is starting to come back full circle and that the separation that once existed between religion and science is beginning to be healed. How very strange that it is in laboratories and not in churches that religious questions are starting to be asked by courageous scientists who are willing to admit that there is a mystery here.

It does seem as if we are moving into a more enlightened age in our scientific explorations as old ways of thinking are crumbling away and being superseded by more intelligent lines of inquiry. And let us not forget that it is often the same questions and the same curiosity that draws people into science as it draws people into the religious life. Some of the best scientific minds in our modern world were deeply religious in their hearts.

So science is not the enemy that must be eradicated; it is just the errors of bad science that need to be allowed to crumble away to dust. But why is it that many of us hold on to the errors of the past and often resist change? If we look through our history we can see that there are many beliefs we once held as true which have not stood the test of time. Yet even though the evidence came forward in a relative instant it seemed to take a long time to assimilate and absorb the new information and to change the beliefs around it. Often it can take generations before the new evidence is accepted. So it seems as if the real problem is not that the scientists of the past produced false doctrines but that we still identify with them today. It is as if we need to feel safe and secure with our impression and understanding of this is how the world is and that this is how the world works. It gives us the foundations which we build our lives upon and which allow us to flourish. But although we don't mind touching things up at the surface in order to give them a new lick of paint, we really resist going back and doing work on the foundations;

even if we know that they are rotten and no longer serve a purpose.

This is why the false doctrines often hang around long after they have become useful and long after they have started to hinder us in our lives because we have outgrown them. The false doctrines of the nineteenth century no longer serve who we are now in this century because we need foundations that reflect our more enlightened and mature state of mind. For the sake of ourselves and for the sake of our planet we need to shake ourselves free of our limitations and to step up and take on the responsibility that has been assigned to us as human beings and as custodians of this world. Like some of the best scientists out there we all need to take that risk.

The Rarest Power of All

Self awareness is the rarest power of all, precious and vulnerable to the highest degree, the supreme and generally fleeting achievement of a person, present one moment and all too easily gone the next. The study of this factor...has in all ages – except the present – been the primary concern of mankind. How is it possible to study something so vulnerable and fleeting? How is it possible to study that which does the studying? How, indeed, can I study the 'I' that employs the very consciousness needed for the study?

Schumacher, A Guide for the Perplexed, p.23.

In reflecting on self awareness it does seem an impossible task to cultivate this quality. How is it that I am capable of stepping out of myself in order to look back towards myself? Does it really make any sense when I say that I am taking the journey into my interior landscape in order to know myself? Am I not in my interior landscape already? If I'm not then where am I?

But a more interesting question that we might ask ourselves is why this small, though extraordinarily difficult, task gives us power and achievement in the world? Why is it so important that we become flexible enough to turn ourselves inwards?

If we look at ourselves intimately we may begin to see how conditioned we are by the circumstances around us. Not only do we have our own personal set of conditions that influences what we think and believe but there are many conditions in the collective consciousness that hold influence and power over us. It is as if we enter many situations and encounter the group mind which tells us what to think and how to act... and mindlessly we obey. It is worth asking ourselves honestly whether there is any thought we have inside of us that is truly original or unique; a thought that has just appeared from nowhere?

When we simply act according to the habit of our circumstances we become powerless no matter how much strength there appears to be in our thoughts and our actions. We are simply the characters in the story who are playing out the script that has already been foreseen and foretold. It is as if we think that there is some God figure up there in the heavens pulling our strings as we move through our day. We are like the well-worn record going around and around stuck in a groove; repeating the same old storylines that we tell ourselves about ourselves. When our lives are like this we may get a strange feeling that everything about the world seems drab and grey. We are just passively reacting to whatever circumstances arise in the same old familiar ways.

It is the rare and precious gift of self awareness that takes us out of this groove and helps us to stand in our power as individuals who can act authentically and can respond to life appropriately in each moment. It is through self awareness that we stop ourselves repeating the same old storylines just as they are about to come out of our mouths and we ask ourselves what really needs to be said in response to this new moment. It is through our self awareness that life appears fresh and new in each second and we are not lazy in applying what we believed in the past to the present situation.

To root ourselves and our lives in self awareness requires a mastery that takes many years to learn. Once it was in monasteries that these skills were learned as the religious seekers were the ones infused with a passion to *know God*. For this is indeed what we are trying to do in gaining mastery of self awareness as we seek to tune in to the God mind inside of us that has the full perspective of the situation and can respond accordingly. It is in accessing the God mind inside of us that we have the possibility to create a life for ourselves.

Yet paradoxically this God mind inside of us is not ours to possess.

It is not limited within the 'I' as a separate entity; but exists beyond it. We cannot control it or hold onto it when we glimpse it. It is the fleeting experience that is present one minute and gone the next. Religious seekers spend a lifetime fervently in its chase and yet may or may not have achieved anything in the process. What do we mean by achievement? What we mean is that one act of creativity that came out of a place of genuine insight.

But although this rare and fleeting thing is hard to pin down; we did take a backward step when we chose to focus our minds on the lesser things that are easier to grasp and control. We refused to stand in our power as human beings who hold rank in the world and we turned our backs on this privileged thing that we had been given. It is time to turn the page and start a fresh chapter. It is time for us to stop acting out our old storylines and to begin the real task of creation.

Rich in Means and Poor in Ends

The result of the lopsided development of the last three hundred years is that Western man has become rich in means and poor in ends. The hierarchy of his knowledge has been decapitated: his will is paralyzed because he has lost any grounds on which to base a hierarchy of values. What are his highest values?

Schumacher, A Guide for the Perplexed, p.58.

We have already looked together at the truth that the highest value which we as humans are here to realise is the value of love. This is the one thing that we have been born to honour above all else. Yet there are many things which we treat as sacred cows that in truth are merely means that are parading as ends.

Quite possibly the biggest sacred cow that we honour is money. It is because of the God of money that we have lost our ground and have become confused as to what is important to us and what is not. It is the God of money that paralyses our will and that causes us to forget that we are here to realise the value of love. Money seduces us off our mission and causes us to remain stuck in a groove of powerlessness.

What is money? Money is nothing more than the price we put on our time. If everyone was willing to give of their time freely there would be no need for money in our society. This is a strange thing for us to consider. Do things really only cost us money because we don't wish to give our time freely? If this is so then why is it then assumed that we won't give our time freely? There are two reasons I can think of as to why we created the system of money. The first reason was to motivate people to give their time to meet the needs of society. It was assumed that individuals would rationally choose to keep their time to themselves and that the needs of society would be neglected. The second reason was to control the abuse of time. It was assumed that if it was given freely that individuals would rationally take more than they needed from another person's time and that there wouldn't be enough to share around for everybody.

Basically it was assumed that love was an end that could not be realised in our society and we created the God of money as a replica. We thought that the God of money would maintain fairness and order in society and we did not trust that these could be established through love. Yet money can never serve as a replacement for love and our free will is paralysed and suffocated by its influence.

For when money dictates how we spend our time we will find ourselves doing things that we really do not wish to do and we neglect the things that are truly important. It is only love that can truly inform us of how our time needs to be spent and where our will needs to be put into action.

Instead we have so much perverseness and insanity that arises by serving the money God. A young mother has to leave her newborn baby in the care of someone else so that she can go out and get a job to pay the bills. An elderly lady has to be put into a home because her children have to go out to work and cannot look after her. I am sure the list is endless.

We are meant to be living in an advanced economic age and yet we still find ourselves having to making sacrifices in order to try and meet our needs. We still feel as if our time is not our own and we spend most of our days concerned with our material survival.

Maybe three hundred years ago it was a necessary step in our evolution to sacrifice ourselves by putting means before ends. Maybe it was more valuable for us then to create an economic system for ourselves that ensured that everyone's time was being put towards the betterment of economic circumstances for all rather than giving individuals the trust that they will know how to manage their own time based on love. It is certainly a risk to give this trust when there are so many individuals who seem so far away from knowing the value of love and who we fear will mischievously create the world of chaos that is least desired.

But when will we ever reach the point of economic stability when we can take that risk if not now? How can we create a society that releases the individual from the straitjacket of money and gives them permission to activate their own will? We cannot look to the authorities to do this for us and to provide us with leadership. Sadly we remain in a situation of fear and more and more smokescreens are being brought down to keep us in service to the money God and to stop us from realising the insanity of our situation. It seems as if we are being discouraged from seeing for ourselves that our time is being spent on things that are not at all important and that we are neglecting the things that are.

If we cannot look to others to help us then we have to help ourselves. But we can only take that risk when we reach the point where we can no longer tolerate the insanity of it all and when we want to reclaim our freedom. When this happens you may be surprised to see that there are invisible forces at work which will keep you safely on this new path you are forging. It seems as if there are higher forces that want to support those who are ready to realise the value of love and who are ready to use their free will by reclaiming back their time. There is truly no need to fear for your own survival if you choose to turn your back on the God of money.

Chiselling your Statue

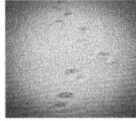

Withdraw into yourself and look. And if you do not find yourself beautiful yet, act as does the creator of a statue that is to be made beautiful; he cuts away here, he smoothes there, he makes this line lighter, this other purer, until a lovely face has grown upon his work. So you do also: ...never cease chiselling your statue[5].

Schumacher, A Guide for the Perplexed, p.64.

The sands are always shifting for us and so it is quite impossible to know thyself by taking one quick look at a particular moment in time. We are dynamic living beings that are never static and are constantly in a state of flux. Every cell in our body is constantly being transformed through a process of renewal and this all happens without us dying at the roots.

This affords us countless opportunities for change. Each moment of our lives, in fact, is a moment for us to create our lives anew. It is a blessing for us that we do not have to go through our lives stuck in the same old groove and do not have to wait for the Day of Judgment after death in order to take a look at ourselves through a life review.

Our statue can be chiselled into something more beautiful each second we are alive. Indeed, every interaction we have with another person, or with the world in general, creates a mirror that reflects back to us where we are at and where we need to cut away here and smooth away

[5] These are not Schumacher's own words but those he quotes from Plotinus in ancient Rome (A.D. 205? -270)

there. But we do not need to be in the world to receive these reflections.

The journey into the interior is one that can be made by choice and is one that can be made by creating some distance between yourself and the world. It is something we can do when we go for a long walk into the wilderness, when we take that silent retreat, or when we simply go to the place where we can have some daily quiet time to ourselves for prayer and meditation. It is fair to say that the first thing that our spiritual practice must create for us is a buffer between the interior and the exterior. It must afford us some space out of the busyness of our daily lives where we can simply stop, withdraw into ourselves, and look. It must be a sacred space that cannot be permeated by outer pressures on our time.

In our modern world it seems even harder now to create this quality time for ourselves where we can withdraw and take that look. Mobile telephones raise the expectation that we are available to the world twenty-four hours a day and the advent of other modern technologies raise the expectation that things must happen instantly at the click of a finger. Finding space for ourselves in the midst of this new world, a space where we are not exposed to the pressures and demands of our lives, is both vital and yet more difficult to achieve. But achieve it we must. Although we ultimately need to reach the point where we can be in the world and to use every interaction to chisel our statue; the permeation must come from the inside out and not from the outside in. We must first learn how to chisel our statue having withdrawn from the world... and then to return.

So how do we find for ourselves a practice that creates a buffer between the individual and their world? How do we create a boundary in a particular space at a particular time that friends and family around us know must not be crossed? How do we create that quality time for ourselves when there is so much pressure to put other people first?

It seems as if many of us have this guilt complex about taking care of ourselves and our own needs. Is it not strange that we are quite happy to run around making sure that the needs of other people are taken care of but we struggle to make a case for taking care of ourselves? We might feel that it is selfish of us to take some time out by withdrawing into ourselves. It gives the impression that we are being indulgent in pampering ourselves rather than it being something absolutely necessary. For in truth we cannot possibly help others if we are not able to help ourselves. We cannot possibly love others unless we first love ourselves.

For what use are we to the world when our statue is chipped and damaged? All we can do in this state is to muddle our way through the best we can. There can be no real power, no authenticity, no creativity, and no love in our actions. Instead the best we can hope for is to try and mimic and live up to some idolised statue of perfection that we may hold in our minds.

The Swinging Pendulum

One of the things we are least aware of in ourselves is our own 'swing of the pendulum.' Other people notice how we contradict ourselves but we do not...It is not as if apparent contradictions were necessarily manifestations of error; more likely, they are manifestations of Truth. Opposites coexist throughout reality, but we always find it difficult to keep two opposites in our mind at the same time...It is my task...to become fully aware of the swing of *my* pendulum...and it is my task not merely to notice the change but to take note of it uncritically, without judging or justifying it. The essence of the task...is *uncritical self-observation*, so that we obtain cool, objective pictures of what is actually happening, not pictures 'retouched' by our current opinions of right or wrong.

Schumacher, A Guide for the Perplexed, p.97.

It is interesting how sometimes we can just catch the moment when our pendulum begins to swing as we are just about to say something that contradicts what we previously said and thought to be true. Often it is the case that we will express an opinion that has gone too far to an extreme and our pendulum will start to swing back to bring us to the middle ground. Yet in order for the pendulum to start to swing we often have to entertain the opposite opinion of what we have just expressed...which creates the contradiction.

How is it possible to keep two opposites in our mind at the same time without becoming crippled by it? There are many areas of our life that do not operate according to straight-line logic where there is only one absolute truth. Many decisions we have to make in our lives require us to somehow balance and grapple with two opposing forces…and we don't seem equipped to handle it. We prefer it when things are straight-forward; we prefer it when things are black or white and clear cut. We prefer it when we can form an opinion in our mind and for that opinion to remain firmly fixed throughout the history of time.

But how does it help us when we see the swing of our pendulum? How are these contradictions manifestations of Truth rather than error? In helps because when our pendulum is swinging it means that we are more open and flexible to the Truth that exists in the present moment. The present moment is always new and virgin; although for many of us we tend to be lazy in attaching old beliefs and concepts around it. It is by force of habit that our pendulum gets stuck and we go around repeating the same old beliefs and opinions about what is happening regardless of whether the situation has changed or not. It is hard work to constantly meet the newness of each moment and each situation afresh. It is hard to keep our minds open to the full spectrum of possibilities of what it is we are observing in that moment.

Instead everything we see in the moment is being retouched by our old beliefs and opinions. We do not entertain the possibility that this moment simply cannot be placed into a drawer in our minds that has already been allocated to it. It is as if we see the sunrise in the morning and immediately it is placed into the drawer with all the other sunrises we have seen in our lives. The uniqueness of this experience of the sunrise is quickly lost on us and the moment passes us by.

But it is when our pendulum is swinging that there is a sense of vibrancy and aliveness in us. Although it appears confusing and chaotic as we jump around in a state of not-knowing we are in fact moving closer to capturing the essence of the moment.

It is hard though to detach ourselves from ourselves so that we obtain the cool, clear pictures of what is actually happening. We have that tendency to move towards the extremes where things can be known rather than staying in that shaky ground of unknowing. We have an aversion to the rawness of the present moment and prefer to translate it in terms of past and future which can be controlled by the mind.

It is to do with letting go of control. To rest in ambiguity and paradox where both opposites can coexist in our mind is a great skill that we
can learn for ourselves as we navigate our way through our lives. It keeps
us flowing in the river rather than tied up on the side of the riverbank.

Yet in truth the moment our pendulum starts to swing we start to
panic and we do what we can to turn a blind eye to it. If someone points
out to us our contradictions we judge and justify it to ourselves in terms
that our mind will grasp and make sense of. We will twist our story and
squirm out of the uncomfortable situation we find ourselves in. We try
and explain away the contradiction so that we can return back to the
certainty of what is known.

To rest in ambiguity, to rest in a place of not knowing, is truly an
uncomfortable place for us to be. But rest here we must if we truly wish
to experience the uncritical self-observation that will truly tell us what is
happening in the moment. In doing so the tide will have been turned.

Directed Attention

All the time, there exists, however, the possibility that I may take the matter in hand and quite freely and deliberately direct my attention to something entirely of my own choosing, something that does not capture me but is to be captured by me. The difference between directed and captured attention is the same as the difference between doing things and letting things take their course, or between living and 'being lived.' No subject could be of greater interest; no subject occupies a more central place in all traditional teachings; and no subject suffers more neglect, misunderstanding, and distortion in the thinking of the modern world.

Schumacher, A Guide for the Perplexed, p.67.

In this meditation we need to ask ourselves to what extent we are living and to what extent are our lives being lived? It does seem to be the case that for most of the time my attention is captured by things that are not of my own choosing. In this way I am doing nothing more than function in the world as I find myself being swept along in a tide that is created and sustained by thought. I receive information through my senses and my ego mind does the work of processing and responding to the information. Nothing new or original can emerge out of the workings of my mind. There is no original thought that exists in the whole world. Every thought I have, every opinion or belief I have formed, has been concocted by forces that are not of my own choosing.

It feels impossible to become free from the world of thought which conditions my every action and things seem to take their own predictable course without any input from myself. Predictability seems to be a curse that hangs over humanity. We all know those types of people who will react in the same habitual ways when you say or do something. With these people we can quite clearly see the functioning of their ego at work as we watch them listen and process the information we give to them. We may be saying something new to them and yet we will see it becoming boxed away in that same place in the mind as something similar we said months ago. When we see that being boxed away in that same place we know that that person is going to react in the same habitual way. He or she is not directing their attention to what we are saying. Indeed how often is it that we feel we are being genuinely listened to and how often do we feel that we are being listened to through the filter of someone's ego?

So how can I possibly free myself from this tyranny? How can I reclaim my life so that I am living it rather than it being lived for me?

The first thing to do is to stop and create some space. When you notice yourself responding to your life in the same old habitual ways; this is the moment to stop and look. Yes you may be driving to work on the same street that you've driven down for the past thirty years but can you stop and see the uniqueness of driving down this street in this precise moment? Can you shift yourself out of autopilot and direct your attention to what is really going on right now?

If we can then this marks the beginning of the end for our ego and it is the moment where we begin to become truly human. However, it doesn't appear to give us very much freedom as human beings does it? For whether I direct my attention to the present moment, or allow it to be captured, I still have to drive down that street to get to my place of work? Most of us are under the illusion of some grand freedom that we might be able to attain where we don't have to go to our place of work at all. We long for the freedom to live our lives as we see fit and we miss the only real freedom that we truly have: namely the freedom to either direct our attention or else have it captured. It is the freedom to choose whether we wish to be held under the tyranny of our mind or not.

It is the same with our economic circumstances. We long for the grand freedom that cuts us free from a life of survival and necessity. We say to ourselves that if we push ourselves today that we will one day reach the point where we no longer have to worry about our economic circumstances. We think that if we push ourselves that we will eventually rise above and gain freedom from it. Yet that day never comes and we find that we are constantly pushing ourselves for more and more. The grand freedom that we crave always seems to be, tantalisingly, just over the horizon. Our attention remains captured and we let things take their course until we reach the time of our retirement when suddenly we look back at a life filled with regrets.

It would be wise of us to turn to the enlightened spiritual teachers of the past who taught that genuine freedom can only be found in the present moment and not in the future. It is right here and now and all it takes is for each of us to cultivate the self-awareness to realise it.

The Greatest Instrument

What enables man to know anything at all about the world around him?...Nothing can be known without there being an appropriate 'instrument' in the makeup of the knower. This is the Great Truth of '*adaequatio*' (adequateness) which defines knowledge as *adaequatio rei et intellectus* – the understanding of the knower must be *adequate* to the thing to be known.

Schumacher, A Guide for the Perplexed, p.39.

We have spoken of this Great Truth in previous meditations but now we must look at it directly. What can be said is that this Truth represents a cornerstone of this book and it is one of the four landmarks to help guide those of us who are perplexed.

Throughout history we find numerous examples of awakened individuals who were misunderstood by those around them. The life of Jesus is perhaps one of the more famous examples to illuminate this point and it is in the Gospel of Mark that we get an illustration of how it was Peter who was the disciple who struggled most in grasping this Great Truth.

For it seems to be the nature of the human condition that the one who has gone to that place beyond the mundane will struggle to return and communicate what it is that he or she has experienced. Words simply cannot capture it because there are no words that are adequate to the task of explaining. Instead it is up to the disciple to raise his consciousness to meet the mind of the teacher in order for understanding to arise of the thing that is to be known.

In the story of the Buddha's enlightenment at the foot of the bodhi tree, he also grapples with the dilemma of how to show and teach what he had experienced with others. For he knew that he had accessed this special hidden 'instrument' inside of himself that was appropriate for the task of gaining full understanding of the thing to be known. Unless those listening to his teaching could also access the same hidden instrument in themselves then his endeavours would be fruitless.

The cornerstone idea of this book is that Fritz Schumacher also accessed the special hidden 'instrument' inside of himself that allowed him to discover certain insights about the human condition. He too faced and grappled with the dilemma of how to communicate these insights with others. Like those who had tried and failed before him he must have felt a sense of despondency and hopelessness at the task that lay before him. That task which all enlightened beings have confronted is the task of bringing about a complete evolutionary shift in human consciousness so that it is the many and not the rare few who are able to access this special hidden instrument and who are able to use it for the benefit of mankind and for the world as a whole.

It is a daunting prospect and it requires great courage and strength of heart to follow this path. Once we have the wisdom, we need a lot of resolve to try again and again to communicate that which cannot be communicated; to try again and again to offer the invitation for those souls who are ready to accept it? There is a real dedication of spirit from those who are committed to the task of a complete evolutionary shift in human consciousness. It also needs the teacher to take a risk in that his teaching and his wisdom may be misused by the follower who is not yet adequate to the task of understanding.

All great pioneers have taken this risk in whatever field that there special instrument is being employed in. Great mystics like Jesus had to take a risk and the consequence was the church. Great scientists like Einstein and Nobel had to take the risk and the consequence were weapons of mass destruction. Great naturalists like Darwin had to take a risk and the consequence was evolutionism. Great explorers like Cook had to take a risk and the consequence was imperialism. Great social commentators like Marx had to take a risk and the consequence was communism. Great religious figures like Gandhi had to take a risk and the consequence was a divided India. And so on.

Yet again and again risks have to be taken in order for humanity to make progress on its own evolutionary path. Despite all the failed attempts to awaken humanity from its slumber, with each passing year there is a sense of progress. More and more people are waking up to the insanity caused by their own limitations and are beginning to make that journey into the interior in order to find that special instrument inside of themselves. More and more people are starting to grow in *adaequatio* and to understand and know a little bit more about the world around them as well as themselves. Gradually more and more of us are starting to get our bearings against this most important of landmarks.

Dealing with Problems

It remains to examine what it means to live in this world. To live
means to cope, to contend and keep level with all sorts of
circumstances, many of them difficult. Difficult circumstances
present problems, and it might be said that living means, above
all else, dealing with problems.

Schumacher, A Guide for the Perplexed, p.120.

We now move swiftly to the fourth landmark that is there to guide
those of us who are perplexed. On the surface this statement appears to
be remarkably gloomy in its perspective on what it means to live in the
world. Where is the joy to be found in life if all we do is spend our time
dealing with problems? It gives the impression that life is tough and hard
work.

Where is the possibility for excelling and gaining freedom when
we are told that the best we can hope for is to keep level in the face of
difficult circumstances? That is because it is not in this world that we can
rise above difficult circumstances and experience joy. The only way to
rise above and experience joy is through our contact with the religious
life.

But my goodness do we try and deal with all our difficult
circumstances in the world so that we can create for ourselves a life of
excellence and freedom. We have come so far in dealing with the

problems of the world and have created the means to eradicate all barriers to our physical health and security. New technology has given us great opportunities to make our lives simpler and effortless and yet despite all this progress we have still been unable to find our freedom in the world. Most people today are devoting the same amount of time to deal with problems as their ancestors did and it is wise to ask whether we will ever reach the point where there are no problems left to deal with by taking this approach? Are our circumstances really any less difficult than those faced by our ancestors?

In some ways our lives are easier it is true. If I think of my ancestors spending twelve hours a day in a mine from the age of ten and compare it to my own upbringing it seems strange to think that my circumstances are not any easier. But the question is whether the things that occupy and concern my mind now are the same as those that occupied the minds of my ancestors?

It was the Buddha who noticed that the first truth about the human situation is that we will experience suffering. I will still have to contend with the same pain of birth, illness, old age and death as my ancestors did. I will still have to contend with the experience of loss and changing fortunes as my ancestors did. Most importantly of all I will still have to contend with the same dysfunctions of ego and economy as my ancestors did.

No matter what we do in the world this situation will not change. We will never be able to eradicate the pain of birth, illness, old age and death no matter how advanced our health care may become. We will never be able to prevent the tide of change from sweeping over and taking away the things that we hold as precious no matter how advanced our immunisation is from the world. And we will never be able to create the perfect ego and the perfect economy that is free from dysfunction in the world.

The only way forward is to find the inner strength and wisdom that allows us to live in the world in the midst of the problems that exist without trying to remove them. This is what the religious life gives to us. For it is in the presence of these difficult circumstances that we cultivate noble qualities like peace, love, trust, acceptance, and openness. These are the qualities that have been locked away inside of us and have been waiting to be opened. It is in the presence of these difficult circumstances that we can pass the lessons given to us in Earth school and to advance and evolve into a Higher State of consciousness.

Rather than gloomily looking at what it means to live in the world in a depressive fashion, we instead focus on the freedom that exists beyond the limitation. Instead of frantically running around trying again and again to kill all these damn problems we focus our time and energy on transcending them completely. In doing so, we will finally become truly human.

A Higher Force

...there is nothing paradoxical in a 'higher' force displaying a
'lower' force, in an experience which is something but *no thing*.
The paradox exists only for those who insist on believing that
there can be nothing 'higher than' or 'above' their everyday
consciousness and experience. How can they believe such a thing?
Everybody, surely, has had some moments in his life which held
more significance and realness of experience than his everyday
life. Such moments are pointers, glimpses of unrealised
potentialities, flashes of self-awareness.

Schumacher, A Guide for the Perplexed, p.78.

It seems a strange idea that it is not in the content or form of the
world that I will find my happiest experiences. We often seem to think
that we must do something or go somewhere in order to have such an
experience. We are dependent on content to give us our pleasure and to
help us avoid pain. But in truth it is not in the things of the world but it is
in that experience of no thing that we find our most significant
moments.

What is this experience of *no thing* that we are talking about here?
It is an experience that is not created out of our sense perception of an
object or the thoughts in our mind about an object. Out of this apparent
emptiness the higher force emerges to displace the lower force and we
stumble upon that glimpse of self-awareness. Have you ever looked up at

the night sky and found yourself stunned into complete silence and awe? If you have then what you are experiencing is the vast nothingness of the universe. It is not accurate to say that you are perceiving space for space has no form or content to perceive. But you are having an experience that feels most significant and real to you.

For it is in the higher force emerging, and in the flash of self-awareness, that you begin to know yourself. Do you really know yourself? Often we define our sense of self by the content of our lives and by the labels and concepts in our mind. We think there is nothing more to who we are than the person who is busily going about their everyday life. But in truth the person who is busily going about their everyday life can never capture the fullness of who we truly are.

The person we think we are in everyday consciousness has been conditioned by so many forces that are determined elsewhere that there is nothing original or distinct to be found in the heart of the person. Every act we perform, and every thought we have, are simply not our own and must have been created elsewhere. We are just the contents of the computer that carries out its predetermined programme and the computer programmer remains nowhere to be seen. It is only when we have an experience of *no thing* that the computer is silent and the programmer can emerge.

How is that the emergence of the programmer guarantees us a more significant and realness of experience than in everyday life? It is as if the programmer allows us to experience our lives in full colour rather than in the dull shades of black & white that our lives were seen through before. The colours may not always be attractive to perceive but we suddenly discover that there is richness in our lives that simply wasn't there before. We are no longer searching to go somewhere or to do something in order to create an experience for ourselves. Instead we have discovered the joy of our 'beingness' which lies at the heart of who we truly are.

Through this joy of being we are happy to have more spaciousness and simplicity in our lives. Our attention is no longer absorbed by the objects of the world that once captured us so completely and we have created some freedom for ourselves. But it is not as if we are looking to become spaced out into some dreamy comatose state through this discovery. We must still live in the world but out of this nothingness the content and form of our lives will be directed with real clarity and with real power from the heart of our being. We will no longer be carried along unconsciously by the ebb and flow of our everyday life and our actions will be infused with newly found creativity and spontaneity.

Then the pointers, the glimpses of unrealised potentialities, will become stronger and stronger until our self-awareness transforms our circumstances for the good of all.

Coming Awake

Now, in order to be aware of where our attention is and what it is doing, we have to be *awake* in a rather exacting meaning of the word. When we are acting or thinking or feeling *mechanically*, like a programmed computer or any other machine, we are obviously not awake in that sense, and we are doing, thinking, or feeling things which we have not ourselves freely chosen to do, think, or feel. We may say afterward: 'I did not mean to do it' or 'I don't know what came over me.' We may intend, undertake, and even solemnly promise to do all kinds of things, but if we are at any time liable to drift into actions 'we did not mean to do' or to be pushed by some thing that 'comes over us,' what is the value of our intentions?

Schumacher, A Guide for the Perplexed, p.68.

In this meditation we continue to explore the theme of what it means to know oneself. What we observe when we begin to become aware is how mechanical we truly are. It can be very hard to admit to ourselves that we spend our lives with our attention largely captured and that we spend our lives doing, thinking, or feeling things which we have not ourselves freely chosen to do, think, or feel.

What force is it that chooses for us what we do, think, or feel? It is strange that many of us may believe that we live in a free and democratic world and that this was the gift that was given to the world by American Independence. We feel soothed by the prospect of the American Dream with the belief that anything is possible and that our destiny lies in our own hands. We also believe in the power of the free market for we think that it gives us the permission to choose for ourselves. In comparison with countries run by dictatorships and/or strict economic controls it seems as if we have got a better deal for ourselves.

Yet is this image of freedom just an illusion; is it a trick that is being played on our minds? For if I can be blunt; *there is no such thing as economic freedom.* The two words are quite simply an anathema against each other. Freedom can only be found once we have *gone beyond* our ego and economy; freedom can never be found *in* ego and economy.

At the root of all forms of economy, even free market economies, lies the assumption of *homo economicus.* Homo economicus is the person we are in ego consciousness and as long as we are that person we will never be free in the true meaning of the word. Yes we may improve the conditions of this prison house and make it more comfortable for ourselves and others; but we will never break free of the prison house altogether.

So what would happen to our economics if we abandoned the assumption of *homo economicus* and entertained the idea that there is more to who we are than our ego consciousness? What would happen is that our economics would be dead; finished with; kaput. For economics has nothing to tell us if we as individuals are awake in the most exacting meaning of the word. If our attention is no longer captured and if we are free to choose what to do, think, or feel then we no longer need to be so obsessed and absorbed with what is going on in our ego and in our economy.

But what is the force that keeps us absorbed with our ego and economy? What compels us to stay in this prison house rather than break free altogether? Is it just a fear of *responsibility*? For if we become awake, and freely choose for ourselves, we will suddenly have to take on the responsibility for our lives. No longer can we plead the defence of ignorance and no longer can we go around and say 'I don't know what came over me.' To be awake in the world is not easy or comfortable because it requires us to become accountable for the intentions we make.

If we freely choose to live consciously in this world we can longer defer responsibility to our God in the heavens above, to our politicians, to our business leaders, to our military leaders.

In truth most of us find it safer to stay in the prison house and to hold on to the illusion of freedom that we have in our minds. Deep down we know that once we take that first step on the journey into the interior that there can be no turning back. Once we embark on the journey of self knowledge, which marks the end of the tyranny of ego and economy over us, we will be alone in the world. What a scary place this appears to be.

But it is *inevitable* that this step into the glorious unknown has to be taken at some time in our lives. Our part in this human story has already been scripted for us. So I ask you; has your time come to awaken?

Those Insoluble Problems

Our civilization is uniquely expert in problem-solving. There are more scientists and people applying the 'scientific' method at work in the world today than there have been in all previous generations added together, and they are not wasting their time contemplating the marvels of the Universe or trying to acquire self-knowledge: they are *solving problems.* (I can imagine someone becoming slightly anxious at this point and inquiring: 'If this is so, aren't we running out of problems?' It would be easy to reassure him: We have more and bigger problems than any previous generation could boast, including problems of survival.)

This extraordinary situation might lead us to inquire into the nature of *'problems.'* We know there are *solved* problems and *unsolved* problems. The former, we may feel, present no issue; but as regards the latter: Are there not problems that are not merely unsolved but insoluble?

Schumacher, A Guide for the Perplexed, p.121.

Although this was written all of thirty-five years ago it remains as true today as it did then. Through time our scientists are able to reduce down the list of unsolved problems but it seems that for every one problem that is apparently solved; another ten are created. Why is this so and why do we not question that in this modern and advanced age we are still dealing with problems of survival?

It is as if we are trying to constantly fit square pegs into round

101

holes. If this is so then is it not just the case that with a bit more time, investment and intelligence that we will get on top of all these problems that are arising? But time, investment and intelligence may have taken us to the moon but they haven't got us any closer to solving the real problems that are a lot closer to our own heart. Is it not time for us to ask whether the scientific method will indeed ever get us closer as it has always promised us it can?

If there are problems that are not merely unsolved but insoluble; then what can we possibly do? Well the first thing we could do is to stop trying to solve them! If you keep running faster and faster despite the fact that your legs are not moving you forward then at what point do you say enough is enough? Do we just try to keep on running even faster and faster and hope that one day we will build enough momentum so that our legs will start to carry us forward? This is madness.

We have an obsession and an addiction in our modern scientific world that is causing us a lot of damage and harm. When faced with an insoluble problem we simply find ourselves adding new layers of complexity to our lives in order to try and deal with it. Often we put in place strange temporary measures just to try and mitigate the worst excesses of the problem at the hand whilst we go away, scratch our heads, and think about how to design a better solution. These temporary measures often themselves create new problems and new temporary measures are put in place to mitigate these…and so on. Before we know it, a complex mess has been created that few can understand. In the modern world a whole new line of employment has been created for those who are able to make sense of the complex situations we find ourselves in…and who quite happily charge to sell their knowledge in the process.

So we never seem able to confront and grapple with the insoluble problems that lie before us. But what is at the root of these insoluble problems? The common factor is the human being himself.

For humans, deep down, are not as static and predictable as a rock. Whilst we are a physiochemical organism, we do not strictly behave according to fixed physical and chemical laws. We cannot create a direct causal chain for predicting human behaviour by saying that if x happens then y will happen. It is because we have an element of free choice that, fundamentally, any problem that concerns human beings becomes insoluble.

Yet all of those who are applying the scientific method to problems of humanity continue to believe that *stable solutions* can be found that apply to all human beings in the world and across an infinite timeframe. Essentially our scientists are trying to eradicate our humanness from the situation and are encouraging us to mimic the behaviour of a rock. Every time that we go against this grain we form new problems for our frustrated scientists who simply cannot pin us down with this limitation. They are forever chasing the impossible dream and it would surely be wise for us to disassociate ourselves from their musings; and to confront and grapple with the insoluble problems that lie before us ourselves.

To confront and grapple with the insoluble problems that lie before us requires the strength of spirit that refuses to eradicate the humanness from the situation. What this means is that we must honour our own humanness in the midst of these problems. We must find that inner courage which seeks the *highest truth* in the situation and we must recognise that the insoluble problem is here to challenge us to bring forth this truth. Schumacher gives the example of how best to school our children as an insoluble problem that requires us to grapple between the giving of discipline and freedom for the child. It is through our willingness to look and grapple (which honours our humanness in that situation) that a higher force of love emerges. It is this force of love that has the power to transcend the problem completely.

Acts of Faith

The level of significance to which an observer or investigator tries to attune himself is chosen, not by his intelligence, but by his faith. The facts themselves which he observes do not carry labels indicating the appropriate level at which they *ought to be* considered. Nor does the choice of an inadequate level lead the intelligence into factual error or logical contradiction. All levels of significance *up* to the adequate level...are equally factual, logical, equally objective, but not equally *real*.

It is by an act of faith that I choose the level of my investigation; hence the saying 'Credo ut intelligam'- I have faith so as to be able to understand. If I lack faith, and consequently choose an inadequate level of significance for my investigation, no degree of 'objectivity' will save me from missing the point of the whole operation, and I rob myself of the very possibility of understanding.

Schumacher, A Guide for the Perplexed, p.43.

In this meditation we will be looking at something that is very difficult to comprehend for someone who is wedded to the scientific method for their investigations. If through a process of logic and deduction you form a conclusion about what you are observing, and in doing so, you remain completely objective in these observations, then how can your conclusion be wrong?

It is hard to comprehend that it is not a question of being right or wrong but that there is something subtle beneath the surface that makes the object of our study so much richer and meaningful than our current level of understanding of it. How can I be correct in what I observe...but yet at the same time completely miss the point of the whole operation?

The idea that it is the faith of the observer that creates understanding is mumbo jumbo to our western minds. We like to think that in our investigations that the observer is a hindrance to the truth and that we can only get to a place of understanding when the observer is completely removed from the picture altogether. This may be true up to a point for it is fair to say that our subjectivity can lead to factual error and logical contradiction.

But it is our ego mind that is the barrier to understanding not the human being in his wholeness. It is our ego mind and all its prejudice that leads to subjectivity. So is it not true then that because we assume that the human being is nothing more than who he is in ego consciousness that we have to eradicate him completely from the investigation?

Yet it is in this assumption that we choose to limit ourselves horribly. It is true that there is the risk of factual error when we allow the human being to be a part of the picture...but there is also the reward of greater understanding to emerge if he can be present and is able to go beyond the limitations of his own ego.

This is where the faith of the observer comes into the picture. It is up to us whether we engage with our investigations through our prejudices or whether we have the faith to look at it through 'the eyes of God'. When we read a play by Shakespeare are we able to attune to the subtlety and deep meaning contained in the work or do we merely hear the 'noise of words on a page'?

It really does beg the question of why we limit ourselves. Why do we close ourselves off to the possibility that our experiences could be richer and meaningful? We either step out of the picture altogether and leave it to the experts to tell us what we are observing or else we step in, bring all our baggage with us, and express our noisy opinions. We cannot see that *wisdom* is a third option that takes us beyond the limitations of both facts and opinions?

Wisdom does not arise out of our intelligence. Our longing for intelligence arises out of *fear* of our own egos. Deep down we don't really wish to be someone who in ignorance spouts off all sorts of opinions that are totally skewed from the truth of the situation we are observing. The price we pay for our fear though is the loss of understanding. Wisdom, on the other hand, can only arise through *love*. Love is nothing other than the conscious self awareness of the object being observed so that its fullness can emerge through our awareness. To cultivate the openness of mind and heart, which allows the fullness of the object to emerge, requires faith in the potential of that object.

Of course in the mineral kingdom there is no potential in that object and so no faith is required in our investigation. But all plants, animals and humans most definitely respond to the love that is given by the observer. All plants, animals and humans most definitely thrive when they are given our consciousness self awareness. In return we ourselves will receive that precious gift of understanding which will be illuminated before our eyes. Then we shall know the true power and significance of faith.

Living Problems

A solved problem is a dead problem. To make use of the solution does not require any higher faculties or abilities – the challenge is gone, the work is done. Whoever makes use of the solution can remain relatively passive; he is a recipient, getting something for nothing, as it were. Convergent problems relate to the *dead* aspect of the universe, where manipulation can proceed without let or hindrance and where man can make himself 'master and possessor,' because the subtle higher forces...are not present to complicate matters. Wherever these higher forces intervene to a significant extent, the problem ceases to be convergent.

Schumacher, A Guide for the Perplexed, p.125.

In this meditation we turn our attention again towards the nature of problems. Here another perspective is given in that solved problems are identified by their *convergence.* This is truly the field of science for manipulation where we work on a problem until it converges towards a stable solution. Through time we get closer and closer to the bottom of the problem until it has been killed altogether. As Schumacher goes on to say *'convergence may be expected...in the fields of physics, chemistry, astronomy, and also in abstract spheres like geometry and mathematics, or games like chess.' (Schumacher, A Guide for the Perplexed, p.125).*

What about the field of quantum physics? Can we expect convergence as we look deeper and deeper into the atom? Apparently not; because when we do so, we only discover its vast emptiness. Quantum

107

physics is not a science in the traditional sense because it is not concerned with the dead aspect of the universe. For this reason quantum physicists need to tread very carefully for they are moving onto sacred ground. It is our quantum physicists today who are asking the same questions as those that were once asked in monasteries and it is they who are observing those subtle higher forces that are present to complicate matters. The wisest physicists know that the rules that apply to the appearance of the physical form cannot be applied to the essence of that form.

So why does the intervention of a higher force cause a converging problem to diverge? We have already looked at the characteristics of a rock and found it is highly predictable because it lacks any inner freedom. It is this lack of inner freedom that allows us to call it dead and that allows us to manipulate it without let or hindrance. What we notice though in looking at this quality of inner freedom is that it arises whenever there is space. It is like pulling a string on a guitar. When the string has been left untouched it has more *space* around it than when it has been pulled. The rock is a form whose string is constantly being pulled whereas we are a form whose string is only being pulled lightly.

It seems therefore that this thing we call space is very important. Yet space cannot really be named because it is not an object that can be perceived through our senses. All we can perceive in that moment is the absence of form. But why is it that in this unpredictable space, where we have complete freedom, that our *movement* is determined by a dualistic framework? Why is it that we have pairs of opposites that set parameters for us of where we can move between? Why is it that the more space and freedom we have, the more these parameters start to spread out?

This is really what we mean by divergence in that the more we look at it, the wider the field becomes. It is as if at first we are in a cooped up pen and the parameters in which we can move are quite small. But as we look more and more it is as if we are let out into a massive field where we can roam much more freely. In truth the more and more we look into something the more we are slowing down the pull of our own guitar string and the more we are creating inner space and freedom for ourselves. Problems that seemed quite straightforward to deal with at first glance suddenly become vast when we put our attention on it.

Of course it is ultimately our own mind that gives us the dualistic framework and sets the parameters where we can move between. It is as if we need to think in terms of 'either this or that' in order to make sense of the world. If something is not black then it must be white. Alas, if our mind is small and petty, and we are lacking in adaequatio, then we will not have much freedom of movement in our own inner space. Or if we choose to let others grapple with these problems then we won't have much inner space either. We might leave it to our church leaders, our politicians, or our scientists to do the exploring whilst we stay safely cooped up in our pen.

But deep down it is up to us to push back these boundaries. Of course there is a risk that, as we push back our frontiers, we will become lost in the vastness of our own inner space. Overwhelmed by the insolubility of the situation we might find ourselves hesitating and unable to move freely. Or else we find ourselves jumping from one side of the fence to the other just to get our bearings straight. However, the ultimate desire for the spiritual seeker is to cultivate his higher faculties and to remove these mind-made boundaries altogether. In doing so they may begin to dwell freely in that awakened state of non-duality.

Into the Inferno

After Dante (in the *Divine Comedy*) had 'woken' up and found himself in the horrible dark wood where he had never meant to go, his good intention to make the ascent up the mountain was of no avail; he first had to descend into the *Inferno* to be able fully to appreciate the reality of sinfulness. Today, people who acknowledge the *Inferno of things as they really are* in the modern world are denounced as 'doomwatchers,' pessimists, and the like.

Schumacher, A Guide for the Perplexed, p.137.

What is the Inferno that we have to descend down into and what is the reality of sinfulness that we need to appreciate? Sinfulness is one of those words that has been skewed and has lost all meaning in our world. But at its root to have sinned simply means that we have missed the mark. Sinfulness is to do with error rather than damnation. Sin is what arises when we live our lives solely in ego consciousness. This is the Inferno.

Why is it pessimistic to acknowledge the truth of the Inferno and the truth of the human condition? If we look at the first teaching of the awakened Buddha we see that he talked about the Inferno. If we look at the life of Jesus we see that he lived to illuminate the Inferno by sacrificing himself on the cross. Acknowledging this is the only way that the mountain can be ascended. There are no short cuts. Yet still we cling on in ignorance and hope. We dream of world peace and harmony and yet we still do not know what it means to find peace in our own hearts.

The ascent up the mountain can only be made when we are free from the tyranny of our own ego and are ready to love. However, it is not by cunning or by force that we wriggle out of our straitjacket but by the light of our self awareness. So we cannot find a cunning and intelligent solution to eradicate all the problems created by our ego and by our economy in order to be free. We may dream of systems that are so perfect that the flawed human condition is completely designed out but they will never be implemented. Yet still we try and create that perfect utopia where there is peace, justice, love and fairness. Or if we cannot think of a cleverer solution we simply try and use force to bring about reform and change. Everywhere we look, we find people actively campaigning and lobbying for a better world and fighting for some particular cause. Everywhere we look there is someone fighting for reform…but it is very rare that we see someone championing a complete revolution.

I am not suggesting that we simply shrug our shoulders whenever we see an act of injustice and tell ourselves that there is nothing we can do to change the situation. Not at all. But the greatest thing we can do first is to simply *look* at the situation. Yet how often do we do this? What it means to really look at the situation is to look through the eyes of complete acceptance that this is what is arising in this moment. It doesn't mean looking through the eyes of ego which is trying to interpret and judge what is arising in this moment with labels of good and bad; right and wrong. Looking through the eyes of complete acceptance means that we are shining the light of self awareness on the situation. A higher force is being engaged and what we really mean is that we are looking on the situation through the eyes of love.

When we look at a situation through the eyes of ego, we can at best only bring about temporary reform. Ego cannot overcome ego. New Economics cannot overcome Old Economics. So when we look at the situation through the eyes of ego we have not descended at all into the Inferno because we still have the screen of ego protecting us and shielding our eyes. We are not allowing ourselves to see the full truth of the situation and we stay in a life of ignorance.

It is interesting that Dante woke up and found himself in a horrible dark wood that he never meant to go. What this really means is that Dante woke up to the fact that he is a part of the human condition and not separate to it. To take responsibility for getting himself out of the horrible dark wood was the first and most important step he could take. This is an act of self love that brings about the end of tyranny from his ego. He is on the journey of awakening to who he truly is.

But it still leaves the question of why he has to go further and descend into the Inferno before he can make the ascent up the mountain? How can looking through the eyes of love *really* bring about a revolution? This is where the power of faith emerges because what happens when you look is that you begin to see that the *seed potential* that manifests the sinfulness in the world lies inside yourself. It doesn't necessarily lie inside your *personal self* who exists in space and time but it most definitely lies inside your *full self in its wholeness.* Through love you begin to transform the seed of sinfulness inside which helps transform the sinfulness in the world. Through this love you ascend the mountain.

To the modern world such talk sounds like nonsense. How can the seed potential for all the sin in the world lie inside of myself? That surely sounds way too heavy a burden to bear on my shoulders. Why should I take responsibility for someone who is carrying out some violent act on the other side of the world? Yet this is what the power of love can do with ease when it flows freely without the hindrance of our own ego. This is the force of grace that we are activating to work through us. But do you have faith in the power of this mighty and transformational force?

Going beyond Thought

It is not a question of good or bad thoughts. Reality, Truth, God, Nirvana cannot be found by thought, *because thought belongs to the Level of Being established by consciousness* and not to that higher Level which is established by self-awareness. At the latter, thought has its legitimate place, but it is a subservient one. Thought cannot lead to *awakening* because the whole point is to awaken from thinking into 'seeing.' Thought can raise any number of questions; they may all be interesting, but their answers do nothing to wake us up.

Schumacher, A Guide for the Perplexed, p.71.

This feels a most powerful statement to meditate upon and it strikes me that it these words that cause me to be wary of our modern western spirituality; because this spirituality remains enthralled by the power of thought. In many respects a lot of the spirituality that is practiced today is immature and is driven by egocentric concern. It expresses what might be called 'the stuff prayer' where we try and plead with our God to give us the stuff that makes our lives more comfortable. One distinction between spirituality and religion that I've heard is that spirituality is to do with the self trying to get God on its terms whereas religion is to do with the God that has us on its terms.

What does it mean to surrender and to allow God to have us on its terms? What it means is that we no longer believe that our thoughts are in charge. We are no longer in the centre of our universe trying to figure everything out and as a result our thoughts quieten down and allow us to awaken into 'seeing.' In surrendering, and out of the silence of our mental chatter, we create space for something new to emerge. We open up and access this mysterious gift of self-awareness; the I Am presence that exists inside of us.

So what are we to do? If we are suffering with an illness is it not wise to use the tools of modern spirituality to heal ourselves by weeding out the bad thoughts and replacing them with good ones? If we are suffering with low self esteem or some other mental block that stops us from realising our potential, is it not wise to weed out the negative beliefs and replace them with positive ones so that our lives can become more successful?

Of course thought does have its legitimate place and yes it is important that we become as healthy as we can in the world. If our anger has caused us liver problems then of course we need to weed out those negative angry thoughts in our mind. This is often why the body develops symptoms of illness to inform us that something is awry with our mind.

But it would be wise for us to remember that we are meddling with some powerful forces here and that often our egos do not know best how to use them. We can only truly know how to use these forces when we are living in a higher Level of Being and where the love of God can guide us. Thought becomes the able servant of awareness rather than its tyrannical master. So if you are using the tools of spirituality to heal yourself, to excel and make it to the top in your field of work, to manifest money, to get a free upgrade on your next aeroplane flight, etc. I would ask you to look and see whether you are coming from a place of love or from a place of fear.

It is very tempting when we are afraid to see these tools and to think that they offer us an easy way out. If we are experiencing a painful illness and are afraid to die then it is natural that our egos will want to do anything possible to get rid of that illness. If we have dedicated our lives to becoming a successful athlete and are afraid to lose then it is natural that our egos will want to do anything possible to win that race. But if we act on this temptation, ultimately, we will only be creating more suffering for ourselves and others even if in the short term we get the quick fix that we are craving.

Let us remember that our primary purpose for being on this earth is to awaken and to remember that all the multitudes of egocentric concerns that we have are purely secondary. Success in life therefore does not exist in time; success can be found in the moment when that moment is cared for in love. Success is found when we awaken to the moment and allow grace to flood through into our lives. So next time you are tempted to open the spiritual toolbox and to create some good positive thoughts for yourself, please ask whether this temptation is coming from love or fear. Is it coming out of the higher force of self-awareness or is it merely coming from the desires of your own consciousness?

Directing Consciousness

Man has powers of life like the plant, powers of consciousness like the animal and evidently something more: the mysterious power 'z'. What is it? How can it be defined? What can it be called? This power z has undoubtedly a great deal to do with the fact that man is not only able to think but is also *able to be aware of his thinking.* Consciousness and intelligence, as it were, recoil upon themselves. There is not merely a conscious being, but a being capable of being conscious of its consciousness; not merely a thinker, but a thinker capable of watching and studying his own thinking. There is something able to say 'I' and *to direct consciousness* in accordance with it own purposes, a master or controller, a power at a higher level than consciousness itself.

Schumacher, A Guide for the Perplexed, p.17.

This is a most remarkable opening definition of the power 'z' that we have been calling self-awareness. It is truly quite incredible to try and imagine this recoiling movement of consciousness upon itself and certainly there is no actual mechanism in our brains that can pinpoint and tell us where this power 'z' exists. I have heard it said before that we can only 'see' this special power in what it illuminates. It is as like a child becoming aware of himself by the illumination of his shadow in the sun or by his reflection in a mirror. Our bodily senses simply cannot give us any direct evidence of our existence as a distinct 'I' that is living in the world.

What a curious a thing to reflect upon but how on earth could it be at all possible for the eye to see itself or for the ear to hear itself? It is also interesting that those dwelling in the animal kingdom are unable to be conscious of their own consciousness. By what force then is an animal motivated to move if it does not have access to this mysterious power 'z'? The only force that can possibly move it is a natural bodily impulse for survival that always seeks to protect the organism. I have heard it remarked that very few wild animals were killed by the devastating tsunami that hit Asia in 2004 and it was as if their bodily impulse led them to higher ground and away from danger. There was no 'I' that was directing the animals to move towards higher ground; *it just happened.*

If this is the case then is this power 'z' not a hindrance for human beings? For as we've developed our own 'I' we seem to have lost touch with the forces of nature and with the bodily impulse for survival. By directing our own thinking we seem to be kidding ourselves by assuming that we can become masters of our own survival and that we do not have to stay in tune with our natural instincts. We have chosen cleverness over intuition; grand plans over impulse.

But the hindrance does not lie with the power 'z' itself but with the misuse of that power. Instead of directing our consciousness towards wisdom and understanding we have surrendered it towards manipulation.

Also, it is wise to remember that although the natural bodily impulse is a powerful force it is still largely reactive more than it is creative. There is no element of choice that is afforded to those in the animal kingdom. The human kingdom is higher because we have that choice. We are the masters who are able to give orders rather than the servants who can simply receive them.

However, we don't seem to have learnt yet how to choose wisely in the orders we give. We haven't learnt how to access the power 'z' in order to bring creativity onto the earth and to be 'the hands and feet of God'. What we have done instead is turn our backs on this mysterious power. We have chosen not to make the effort of becoming aware of our own thinking and have chosen instead to remain a slave of our own consciousness. We have been bestowed with the privilege of being born into this human form and of having dominion over the world but we haven't yet grown into the role that we've been assigned.

There are many archetypal stories about the immature king who only brings suffering to his kingdom because he cannot handle the power and responsibility he has been afforded. Maybe it is meant to be the way of things that we have to learn on the job and to learn through our mistakes rather than being primed and made ready for the role beforehand.

But are we really learning through our mistakes? Our material circumstances may be more favourable now than at any other time, but even so, the observations that Jesus and the Buddha made about the human condition more than two-thousand years ago remain just as relevant today. When is the moment going to come for our awakening?

The Suprahuman Level

Jakob Lorber, Edgar Cayce, and Therese Neumann were intensely religious personalities who never ceased to aver that all their knowledge and power came from 'Jesus Christ' – a level infinitely above their own. At this suprahuman level, each of them found, in their various ways, liberation from constraints that operate at the level of ordinary humanity – limits imposed by space and time, by the needs of the body, and by the opaqueness of the computer-like mind. All three examples illustrate the paradoxical truth that such 'higher powers' cannot be acquired by any kind of attack and conquest conducted by the human personality; only when the striving for 'power' has entirely ceased and been replaced by a certain transcendental longing, often called the love of God, may they, or may they not, be 'added unto you.'

Schumacher, A Guide for the Perplexed, p.93.

These words trickle through me like a soothing balm trickling down on an open wound. They simply ooze and resonate with the voice of the spirit and surely come through the mind and hands of one who has seen.

The life and story of these three individuals is not our concern in this meditation; our focus rests instead on the paradoxical truth that has been illustrated. For the 'attack and conquer' approach is the one we do seem to hold onto quite tightly whether it is with regards our relationship to the world or even our relationship to ourselves. It strikes me that when we take the journey into the interior to attack and conquer our darkness that we are not being very loving towards ourselves. It is not through the power and force of the personality that the faults of the personality can be overcome and yet despite this many of us are indeed trying to follow this path of self development and improvement.

The first stage of loving oneself requires our complete acceptance of what is happening now. What this means is that we are looking at ourselves through the eyes of awareness rather than through the eyes of the personality. Fundamentally the personality is constantly dissatisfied with the reality of the present moment and is always trying to escape from it in some form or other. Rather than being with what is we instead focus on our future goals and try and attack and conquer the present moment in order to get there. This may bring some form of success but it is clearly not a healthy form of development and growth for the self.

We seem to live in an age where there is a constant fear of failure that is hanging over us. Our lives revolve around 'keeping up appearances' and of trying to meet the expectations of others. It seems as if there are few people in the world who are truly comfortable being themselves; who have truly accepted who they are.

Not only are these few people able to stop trying to attack and conquer themselves but they are able to stop trying to attack and conquer the world around them too. In releasing this striving for power they too may suddenly discover in themselves this transcendental longing, the love of God, which is where the true force of power emerges. This power, enacted by love, is truly a transformative, restorative and healing force that brings about real change.

How paradoxical it is that we have to learn to accept the present moment before genuine change can arise. How strange it is that we have to *appear* to be meek and passive in order to be a real catalyst for action.

To recognise this paradox is a real act of faith in something that is beyond the personality and beyond words. As these three individuals found their faith in 'Jesus Christ' we too have to find our faith in a force that can truly liberate us from the constraints of ordinary humanity.

We are on an island and on that island we seem to be very comfortable with our lives. We have attacked and conquered every last inch of that island and gained every worldly power that is possible to gain. But we are still limited by our fear of the deep waters that surround our island and it is our fear that imprisons us. These are the limits imposed by space and time, by the needs of the body, and by the opaqueness of the computer-like mind. It requires a real leap of faith for us to surrender and dive off the island into the vast ocean. Such a leap of faith will naturally arise when we become aware of our transcendental longing and when we realise that the things of the world no longer have any power over us. Such a leap of faith naturally arises when love overcomes fear.

Why is it that we are afraid of the deep waters of the ocean? We are afraid because it is unknown and uncertain what will emerge once we take that dive. On our island we feel safe with the familiar surroundings we find ourselves in. On our island we like to kid ourselves that we are free to move where we choose and that we can conquer all. When will we wake up to the fact that this impression of freedom is nothing more than a fanciful dream?

The Power of Forgiveness

The steadily advancing concentration of man's scientific interest on 'sciences for manipulation' has at least three very serious consequences...

...Thirdly, the higher powers of man, no longer being brought into play to produce the knowledge of wisdom, tend to atrophy and even disappear altogether. As a result, all the problems which society or individuals are called upon to tackle become insoluble. Efforts grow ever more frantic, while unsolved and seemingly insoluble problems accumulate. While wealth may continue to increase, the quality of man himself declines.

Schumacher, A Guide for the Perplexed, p.56.

The first two consequences referred to in this quote have been considered in depth throughout this book. In this meditation I felt to focus on the third and on this issue of *atrophying*.

It is enough to leave one feeling somewhat in a state of despair to know that not only have we failed to use the right tools in our toolbox; but that these tools have now gone rusty or appear to have disintegrated altogether. How can we possibly arrest this gloomy situation?

The only way forward for us is to build faith and trust through the power of *forgiveness*. However, we need to tread very carefully here as forgiveness is another loaded word in our vocabulary that seems to sit comfortably, or should I say uncomfortably, in tandem with the other loaded word of sin. With this in mind, I have heard it said that there can be no forgiveness without first finding a healthy expression of anger. If someone or something has crossed our boundary then it is not enough to meekly say I forgive without first acknowledging and expressing the anger that inevitably arises whenever a boundary has been crossed.

So what is it that we need to be angry about? What boundary of ours has been crossed? Well I think it is fair to be angry about the situation and circumstances we find ourselves in at the moment. We were born as human beings and yet we seem unable to express and voice our real humanity without being treated somewhat oddly by those around us. Our questions about the meaning and purpose of man's existence are ignored and waved away by our peers and there seems to be no-one we can turn to for advice. We are simply crying out for elders who can offer us leadership and help us grow into our wholeness and yet none are forthcoming. Instead our innocence is being taken away from us at a very young age as we find ourselves being groomed into a world of scientism and rationality. Success is measured by the extent to which we can carry out instructions and not by the strength of our love.

Yet we feel uncomfortable when asked to face the truth and instead we cling on to the illusory ideas of freedom and democracy. What does it help us to have freedom of choice in the world when we don't even have any freedom in our own thoughts? When we finally face the truth of our impoverishment there are many things that we can be angry about. But it is in finding a way to honour and work with our anger in a healthy manner that we may eventually come to a place of peace and forgiveness for the human condition. We have to learn to accept and forgive the circumstances that created the atrophying of these higher powers of man before we can start afresh.

The life and story of Jesus is all about the restorative power of forgiveness. Here was a man who came down onto this earth, turned the other cheek and bore the full force of the human condition upon his shoulders, and yet, in spite of all this, was able to express his final words of forgiveness before his death on the cross.

Likewise it is only through the power of our own forgiveness that transformation occurs *and our higher powers are restored.* We have to be there observing those around us, who run hither and thither, and who frantically try and tackle the insoluble... and simply offer our forgiveness.

But if we have not honoured and worked with our anger and frustration first then this act of forgiveness may never arise. The energy of our anger will spill out and we will join the crowd of people who grow frantic trying to change their circumstances and who try to solve all the problems that cannot be solved. As long as our anger is left to spill outwards the atrophying of our powers will continue and there will be no true restoration from within.

If you look closely you will often see that those who are vying for reform are angry about something. It is indeed rare to find someone who is itching for change whilst maintaining peace in their heart. Everyone it seems is aware of some injustice in the world that they wish to protest against and which they hope can be eradicated through the frantic outpouring of their anger. I am not suggesting that we stand back with a shrug of gloominess at the state of the world and the human condition. But let us remember that no lasting remedy can be found through the energy of anger and that this outpouring will not arrest the decline in the quality of man. There have been millions of reforms put in place over the years and yet still we face the same problems of the human condition. When will we learn to move through our anger and find this mysterious transformative power of forgiveness? When will we unlock the right door and bring about real change?

On Evolutionism

Chance and necessity and the utilitarianism of natural selection may produce curiosities, improbabilities, atrocities, but nothing to be admired as an *achievement* – just as winning a prize in a lottery cannot elicit admiration. Nothing is 'higher' or 'lower'; everything is much of a muchness, even though some things are more complex than others – just by chance. Evolutionism, purporting to explain all and everything solely and exclusively by natural selection for adaptation and survival, is the most extreme product of the materialistic utilitarianism of the nineteenth century. The inability of twentieth-century thought to rid itself of this imposture is a failure which may well cause the collapse of western civilization. For it is impossible for any civilization to survive without a faith in meanings and values transcending the utilitarianism of comfort and survival, in other words, without a religious faith.

Schumacher, A Guide for the Perplexed, p.115.

Schumacher is not mincing with words in this very strong statement that we will be meditating upon. Therefore this is not something that is easy for us to chew and digest without stirring some resistance inside of our guts. This is a tough issue for us to look at squarely and honestly and it seems as if it is an act of cowardice on our parts that has allowed this imposture to remain throughout the twentieth, and now into the twenty-first, century.

125

Why does the doctrine of evolutionism stir such anger and wrath? In our previous meditation we looked at this energy of anger and now it seems as if we have to get down into the root of it. For at the heart of all that there is to be angry about in the world we find evolutionism at work. We find that it is the doctrine of evolutionism that has brought about an incessant reductionism in our religious life to the point where we no longer feel the urge to honour it.

Traditionally it was in the religious life that we were led from the everyday and ordinary to something that was higher and greater. There was a clear distinction between the two and there was a sense of achievement that arose when an individual progressed on the path between the two. The sense of achievement naturally arose from having taken responsibility and care for one's life and having found meaning in it.

But through the doctrine of evolutionism that distinction was eradicated and it was replaced with a belief that every aspect of our lives is geared solely for survival. Why is this belief so damaging? It is so damaging because it denies that there is any significant distinction between the animal and human kingdoms. We may be able to learn a lot *about* humans by observing the behaviour of animals but what we fail to notice is their humanness. Yes, on one level we are here on this earth to ensure our survival, but on another level, we are here for a much higher purpose.

It is said that the doctrine of evolutionism emerged from the work by Charles Darwin in the mid-nineteenth century and it would be easy to point the finger of blame at him for having brought this belief into the world. Such an act would be unwise for Darwin himself knew that his observations of the animal kingdom needed to be placed in a much broader context. Namely his observations needed to be put in their appropriate place as subservient to religion and not as their replacement. What difficulties he grappled with in publishing his work for he clearly knew that lesser men than he would not have the wisdom to hold his observations in this broader context. If he knew this then why did he go ahead and publish his work? It is because he knew that his work had been created for a purpose, and that even if it led to us taking a backward step at first, then ultimately it would help us find our way.

It is strangely true that the doctrine of evolutionism that emerged has shown and illuminated for many of us the value and importance of the religious life whereas in the age before evolutionism it was probably taken for granted. It is somewhat queer that we often only value something in its absence and only after we have lost it. The emergence of a growing interest in spirituality and religion in the western world these past fifty years has come, I feel, *because* of the doctrine of evolutionism. It has shown to us very clearly that our civilisation can no longer survive without a faith in meanings and values that transcend the utilitarianism of comfort and survival.

Oh how odd it is though that we have to reach a crisis point before we can find our way again. Oh how odd it is that we have to reach a crisis point before we can begin to look honestly and find our courage. We have to have our pot stirred by some event or circumstance in order to find our strength to meet it. The story of Tibet is one that comes to mind here. This was a country that was once insulated from the outside world and whose comfortable religious way of life was taken for granted. Yet it was a country that needed the invasion of the Chinese authorities, and the threat this posed to the Tibetan way of life, in order for the true power of their religion to emerge in response. In adversity the Tibetan culture has actually gained strength and in doing so it has also helped bring the gifts of Buddhism to the west. Likewise we too have to work with the anger that is stirred by the invasion of evolutionism in our lives and to draw on our religious faith to work through it and respond appropriately. It is time to look at the truth about evolutionism and to see it for what it truly is.

A Faith Destroyed

Evolutionism is not science; it is science fiction, even a kind of hoax. It is a hoax that has succeeded too well and has imprisoned man in what looks like an irreconcilable conflict between 'science' and 'religion'. It has destroyed all faiths that pull mankind up and has substituted a faith that pulls mankind down.

Schumacher, A Guide for the Perplexed, p.114.

It seems as if we are not quite ready to let go of our wrath towards the doctrine of evolutionism and that there is still something left for us to chew upon in this meditation. We are coming towards the end of our time together in this work and it is perhaps helpful for us to recall what we are trying to achieve together through these meditations. I have also been thinking a lot recently about the command of Jesus where he urges us to seek first the kingdom of God and to trust that all else will then be added.

In Christian terms, it was in the story of Adam and the Garden of Eden where it is said that the fall of man began. For Adam chose to go it alone by taking the forbidden apple and in doing so cut his ties from the kingdom of God. Adam, so we are told, caved in to the temptation to put the things of the world first and it marked the loss of his faith. Yet if this archetypal story is to be completed then one day man must begin to turn around and come back home to the kingdom. After the fall of man must come the rise of man and it is the command of Jesus that we will hear whenever we are ready to turn around.

Now I can tell that Schumacher was impatient for that time of the grand turning – not just of himself but the whole of humanity - to come in his lifetime and it seems as if he saw the doctrine of evolutionism as the one force that was standing in the way of this momentous event in human history. It is a force that exists to drown out the voice of Jesus' command and that exists to bar our return to the kingdom.

Yesterday we spoke that strength can arise out of adversity and that in the dying embers of evolutionism we may one day begin to really appreciate the religious life. In seeing its emptiness we will one day long for a life that is much richer and meaningful. We will one day see that it was nothing more than a mischief maker that had stirred up trouble by creating an irreconcilable conflict between religion and science that did not need to exist.

But today I come with a different message. This message is that we do not need to wait until for the end of evolutionism before we can begin the journey home. I have heard it said recently that we mistakenly think that peace can only happen in the absence of war. I heard instead that peace is a higher force that completely transcends war; which means that peace can be found even right in the midst of war. Peace is a quality that rests in the heart and which need not be affected by outer circumstances unless we choose to allow it. Peace can be found in simply honouring our existence with each breath. Likewise the kingdom of God rests within the heart of each and every one of us and we can return home regardless of the outer circumstances. Are we willing to make this choice; even in the presence of this hoax?

Schumacher's wrath towards the doctrine of evolutionism gives it a power that it simply does not have on its own. By putting attention on it the hoax becomes real. By taking it too seriously the hoax becomes significant. Instead we would be wise to simply treat it for the joke that it is. That is to treat it lightly and with a sense of humour rather than with a sense of indignation. I mean it is rather funny is it not that we have allowed ourselves to believe that we are nothing better than a slightly more complex and intelligent ape? For anyone who has gone deep inside and who knows themselves and have experienced life, even if it is just a smidgen, will surely tell you that this belief is rather laughable. No matter how clever or intelligent the argument is being put to us, those of us who have seen will know the truth of this hoax.

When you watch the news tonight and hear all these stories of drama and trauma that only tell you tales about the fall of man I would advise you to not take these too seriously and instead give a knowing smile that there is a mischief maker at work here. For why is it that stories of genuine faith never make it onto the news? It is because we are lost in a vicious cycle and the record that is playing has become stuck on a groove. The doctrine of evolutionism, that we so believe in our minds, is reinforced by what we tell ourselves about our world. If our faith tells us that man is locked into a competitive struggle for survival then this is the news that we will want to hear in order to reinforce that message. We certainly do not want to hear stories that tell of the rise of man, and even if there is someone we know who meets that description, we will unconsciously long for them to fail. How bizarre it is that we will go to such lengths in order to try and preserve our outdated beliefs about the fallen state of humanity.

We would be wise then to detach ourselves from this insanity and go our own way. If you look you will easily find plenty of sources of inspiration out there that can help you hear Jesus' command and that can help you take the journey into the interior. Turn your ears away from the noise of the mischief maker and go ahead and listen to that call.

Limitless Potentialities

This 'open-endedness' is the wonderful result of the specifically human powers of self-awareness, which as distinct from the powers of life and consciousness, have nothing automatic or mechanical about them. The powers of self-awareness are *essentially* a limitless potentiality rather than an actuality. They have to be developed and 'realized' by each human individual if he is to become truly human, that is to say, a person.

Schumacher, A Guide for the Perplexed, p.22.

We move swiftly now from the limited to the limitless. To recognise the open-ended potentiality can though be a shocking and dangerous experience for us to bear. We are like the frog who has spent his whole life in the confines of a well and who steps out and discovers the vastness of the ocean. It is truly overwhelming and in the story of the frog his head simply explodes because he cannot quite comprehend the open-endedness. We are also like the individuals who have spent the whole of their adult lives imprisoned or in the confines of a monastery and who on returning to the outside world are unable to cope with the change. Institutionalisation is a disease that is going to be hard to heal.

Specifically we are not used to thinking for ourselves and of standing on our own feet. From a young age we have learnt to let others do the thinking for us and we rest in the assumption that they know what they are doing and where they are going as we follow in their footsteps. Little do we know that those who do the thinking for us are not necessarily the ones who have learnt to think for themselves and who know where they are going.

There are those who have gained the wisdom from having learnt to think for themselves and what is quite clear is that they do not tell other souls to follow them blindly. They instead walk freely and spontaneously on their own path and they urge others to do the same. For there is nothing automatic or mechanical about their lives and they cannot give us a magic formula to put into practice. There is, quite simply, no set of instructions to follow when your life is governed by the force of self-awareness.

But it is hard for us to hear that these limitless potentialities have to be developed and realised ourselves and that no-one will be there to do the work for us. Alone in this world we have to take those baby steps and learn how to walk in our own shoes.

Why is it that we choose to live in limitation within the world of consciousness rather than break free into the limitless world of self-awareness? Why do we resist the fact that we have born as a human being and that as long as we have breath inside of us we have these limitless potentialities at our fingertips? Why do we deny the truth of who we really are and deny the yearning of our own beating heart?

It is because we are afraid and lack the courage. With no enthusiastic cheerleaders backing us we instead risk the cold shoulder of the world when we choose to walk our own path rather than follow the crowd. Our controversial actions will only provoke ridicule and condemnation by those who are unsettled by the sight of someone walking randomly in a different direction. It takes a very strong and courageous person to take this risk and to honour the yearning in their own heart. But the time will surely come when all of us will have to take that leap of faith and to leave behind a mechanical life that no longer satisfies us. Strangely it is quantum physicists today who also talk to us about the open-ended potentialities that lie before us and that life is not as fixed and determined as we once thought.

What will it take for you to realise the 'mechanicalness' of your existence? What will it take for you to realise that you have been institutionalised into a confined world of limitation. Yes, if you live in certain countries, you may have freedom of expression, the freedom to travel anywhere in the world, to live where you like, to marry who you wish. But is this freedom real? If our minds have been programmed to operate mechanically and have been programmed so that we automatically step in line with the crowd then do we really have freedom of expression and freedom to go anywhere? If we can't even think for ourselves and to act according to the feelings of our own heart then how can we possibly call ourselves free?

At some point in your childhood you would have taken on board certain assumptions about who you are and about what your place is in the world. Your whole education and upbringing gave rise to so much conditioning in your mind that there is not one unique thought that arises in it. The only uniqueness we have rests in the feelings of our heart and the thoughts and impressions that come to give form to those feelings.

So we go through our lives thinking that we are free and that there is an open-endedness of choice available to us. We can go and live and work in this town or that town. We can go and shop for our groceries here or we can go there. We can go and marry this person or that person. We can conceive and raise one child or two. We can study and train in one profession or another. We can elect this politician or that. Our lives are run according to a list of objectives that we try and fulfil. If that list is met then we think to ourselves that our potentiality has been realised.

But in truth we need to ask ourselves whether it is the yearning of our heart that informs this list or whether they are simply a list of expectations that are designed to help us find a comfortable place for ourselves amongst the crowd?

Moving into Greatness

It is not truly difficult to appreciate the difference between what is alive and what is lifeless; it is more difficult to distinguish consciousness from life; and to realize, experience and appreciate the difference between self-awareness and consciousness is hard indeed. The reason for the difficulty is not far to seek: While the higher comprises the lower and therefore understands the lower, no being can understand anything higher than itself. A human being can indeed strain and stretch toward the higher and induce a process of growth through adoration, awe, wonder, admiration and imitation, and by attaining a higher level expand its understanding. But people within whom the power of self-awareness is poorly developed cannot grasp it as a separate power and tend to take it as *nothing* but a slight extension of consciousness. Hence we are given a large number of definitions of man which make him out to be *nothing* but an exceptionally intelligent animal with a measurably large brain, or a tool-making animal, or a political animal, or an unfinished animal, or simply a naked ape.

Schumacher, A Guide for the Perplexed, p.21.

We are coming to the end of our time together and in this final meditation we still find ourselves at the crossroads. In one direction lies the road that is familiar to us and is the one we have been walking on since the time of Adam. In the other direction lies the road that can lead

134

us home to the kingdom. This is the choice that lies before us.

But to take the road home we need to grasp that this thing we have been calling self-awareness does really exist as a separate power and that it is absolutely distinct from the power of consciousness. But still we do not know how to strain and stretch ourselves in order to recognise that which is higher and to expand our understanding.

This is why the art of discipleship is so important because it is through discipleship that we can begin to induce a process of growth through adoration, awe, admiration and imitation. To be a disciple is to be someone who has the faith that there is a teacher and a teaching that is higher than oneself. To be a disciple is to be someone who recognises the one who has gone beyond to the other shore and who is willing to believe that what the teacher is trying to express is distinctly different from what is being expressed by the rest of the crowd. To be a disciple is to be someone who recognises that we are at a crossroads and who looks for the one who has followed the road less travelled; who looks for the one that has taken that unfamiliar road back home.

This is a paradox that lies before us. On the one hand the choice lies within us and we are alone in making that choice and in walking our own path. Yet on the other hand we need to hear and be reassured by those who have gone to the other shore before we can find the courage to take that journey home. It is as if those who have gone to the other shore are available to help us access the whisper of our own beating heart that has been there all along. They inspire us to feel it by steadily illuminating that which is higher; by steadily illuminating this mysterious power of self-awareness. They show us that it is truly possible to live freely and without limit in that quieter place that exists beyond the ruminations of our own ego.

But the master can only invite and can never impose on his disciples. All of us at some point in our lives will reach the point of exhaustion with the road that has been so familiar to us. We will all one day reach the point of exhaustion with our world of ego and economy and our thirst will no longer be satisfied with the definitions of man that have been given to us. It is only at this point of exhaustion that we will begin to hear the invitation that has always been there waiting for us to accept. Although it may feel as if we have been walking mechanically on this one road for eternity, in truth, we do not realise that every step we take brings us to a crossroads and offers us a way out. With our blinded tunnel vision compelling us to trudge on that same old road we simply do not see the alternative.

How strange it is that the one thing that we have been always searching for is the one thing that has always been here. In the ups and downs and changing fortunes of our lives this thing we have been yearning for has remained as a constant presence deep inside. It is truly closer than close and yet despite this we push it far, far away from us. We build a fortress between ourselves and this thing and in the process our special power of self-awareness diminishes and fades. How truly sad it is that this happens but how absolutely necessary it seems to be that we have to go through this process of building this fortress and then tearing it down again. It is all a part of the human story. The ultimate question is whether you are ready yet to tear down your fortress of ego and to feel the quiet whisper of your beating heart?

Afterword

I am truly grateful to have had this precious time of contemplation with the Guide these past forty days. It feels as if in the process I've been giving the seed inside of me some of the watering it needs in order for it to shoot and grow. It is nourishing to remind myself of the choice that is always there before me and to satisfy the thirst inside that longs to take that road back home to the kingdom.

Fritz Schumacher's wise words have always had the power to soothe and heal like a drop of balm on an open wound. These words also have the power to cut right through my ego and to enter into the sacred chamber of my heart where its resonance helps resuscitate me to life. This lineage of wisdom that he embodied and expressed shows to me what is truly important.

I hope that through these meditations you too have caught a glimpse of its power and that you are inspired to accept the invitation of awakening too by taking that same road home. I especially hope that these meditations have stirred your curiosity and interest in this work so that this special little book can be brought back to life and into our awareness once more. May this book come alive again to help give us the courage we need to face the time of the grand turning with confidence and with grace.

Thank you for your purchase of this book.

Author's rely heavily on customer feedback for marketing and promotion of their work. You are warmly encouraged, therefore, to provide a review on the sales channel for this book; on the Amazon website.

About the Author

R.A. Moseley is an English writer currently living in Margaret River, in the South-West corner of Australia, with his wife Melissa and his cat Grace.

His mission in life is to be a spiritual friend; one who uses the power of the written word to illuminate that there is far more going on beneath the surface of our day-to-day human existence.

Tracking Fritz's Footsteps: Meditations on E.F. Schumacher's A Guide for the Perplexed is the second of four publications to his name. Other titles are:

The Search for Satya (2012)

The Kingdom of Golf is Within You (2014)

and

Hamartia (2018)

All titles are self-published through Create Space; with print and e-book copies available for purchase through Amazon and other online distributors.

www.ingramcontent.com/pod-product-compliance
Lightning Source LLC
Chambersburg PA
CBHW031851090426
42741CB00005B/451